Be
Your
Best!

The Quest Toolbox Series

This series is different. It provides practical techniques, tested by experienced consultants with real organisations. Each tool follows a step-by-step approach, illustrated by worked examples. No theoretical explanations, just a wide choice of techniques to help stimulate, drive and manage change and the people that create it. Hundreds of directors, managers and team leaders worldwide are already using the series for personal reference, as handout material for training programmes or as an aid for project or improvement teams.

Steve Smith

Dr Smith has been helping organisations transform their performance and culture for 20 years. His unique experience of witnessing and consulting in global corporate change has helped him become regarded as one of the most progressive change management consultants of his generation.

A regular speaker and author, as well as conceptual thinker, Steve has facilitated the metamorphosis of over 150 organisations through the provision of timely, supportive and often pioneering consultancy advice.

A strong advocate of an holistic approach to business improvement, Steve works with his clients to define stretching, yet balanced strategies that work, and then helps to mobilise the whole organisation to turn those strategies into action.

Prior to forming Quest, Steve was a director of PA Consulting Services, where he worked for 11 years and founded the TQM division. A former lecturer at Aston University, Steve has also spent eight years with the Chrysler Corporation.

Acknowledgements

The Toolbox series has been drawn from the expertise of the entire Quest Worldwide consultancy team. Special thanks must go to Gillian Hayward for selecting and compiling tools for all five titles and to Mike Rayburn who developed and refined many of the techniques in *Make Things Happen!* Thanks also to Peter Holman, Tina Jacobs, Sue Hodder and the Quest support team.

Be Your Best!

Readymade Tools for Personal Development

Edited by
Steve Smith

YOURS TO HAVE AND TO HOLD
BUT NOT TO COPY

First published in 1997

Kogan Page Limited
120 Pentonville Road
London N1 9JN

© Quest Worldwide Education Ltd

British Library Cataloguing in Publication Data

A CIP record for this book is available from the British Library.

ISBN 0 7494 2481 8

Typeset by Florencetype Ltd, Stoodleigh, Devon
Printed in England by Clays Ltd, St Ives plc

Contents

Introduction

*"You can't manage others
until you can manage yourself."*

Now perhaps more than ever we are expected to be responsible for ourselves. Not just for our families and interests, but for our career development, job satisfaction and personal fulfilment. Understanding and managing yourself is a vital skill for everyone – enabling you to contribute more effectively at work and at home.

This Toolbox provides you with tools to help you understand yourself and to build a more fulfilled future. No-one ever claimed the road to personal success and fulfilment was easy but this Toolbox will help give a framework to your thoughts.

How to use this Toolbox

What it is

This Toolbox is designed to help you make the best of yourself.

It will help you to:

- know yourself
- plan your life
- develop yourself
- get organised
- work well with others
- present yourself well
- welcome change

by providing you with easy, practical tools you can use on yourself, by yourself.

How to use it

1. Decide on your particular area of need.
2. Choose the relevant section in the index.
3. Browse through the tools.
4. Decide which tool to use.
5. Turn to the detailed tool description. The 'What it is' section explains the purpose of the tool; the 'How to use it' section gives you step by step instructions, and the 'How it helps' section outlines the benefits of using the tool.
6. Just do it!

How it helps

Self-development is a never ending journey. It can be daunting and difficult. This Toolbox will help you by breaking your journey into achievable steps and giving you practical tips and methods for passing the milestones along the way.

IT ALL STARTS WITH BELIEF.
IF YOU THINK YOU CAN, YOU WILL

Tools index

1 Know yourself

Find Out How You Think?

What it is

Our brains are divided into quadrants which each have different functions and abilities:

Right frontal: best at creative tasks and ideas. It deals with pictures rather than words, seizes on novelty and is keen on metaphors.

Right basal: deals with feelings and intuition. Compassion, interest and concern for others are rooted here.

Left frontal: best at logic and reasoning. Includes problem solving, strategic vision, leadership and decision-making skills.

Left basal: best at organising the world; sorting, arranging and filing; keeping order and maintaining routine.

Each of us possesses all four to some extent and 95% of us use some parts more than others. Generally men tend to use more of their left brain; women more of their right.

This questionnaire, developed by Katherine Benziger, will help you assess how you think.

How to use it

1. Read the statements in each section and tick those you feel apply to you.

Do not tick statements which describe things you have to make an effort to do, only those which come easily.

Left frontal

- [ ] I prefer to have the final say in family money matters
- [ ] I am logical and tend to think in straight lines
- [ ] I love machines and enjoy using tools
- [ ] I like delegating and giving orders
- [ ] I like to be able to measure my success objectively – it is not enough just to be happy about what I'm doing
- [ ] I feel comfortable working with figures
- [ ] I enjoy verbal arguments. I like to get my ideas across
- [ ] I tend to take responsibility for big decisions
- [ ] I am good at technology
- [ ] I value effectiveness in other people
- [ ] People often look to me for leadership
- [ ] If there's a problem, I can usually see what is causing it and come up with an answer
- [ ] I am good at managing money
- [ ] I enjoy DIY
- [ ] I believe thinking is more important than feeling.

___

Total left frontal

Right frontal

- [ ] I use a lot of hand gestures when I talk
- [ ] I like to work on several things at once
- [ ] I often come up with new inventions
- [ ] I often rely on hunches to solve problems
- [ ] I get some of my best ideas when I'm not thinking about anything in particular
- [ ] I am very energetic
- [ ] I am artistic
- [ ] I like to use metaphors and visual analysis to explain and understand things
- [ ] I get excited by off-the-wall ideas
- [ ] I always 'file' things in stacks rather than in cabinets
- [ ] I tend to be more interested in the 'big picture' rather than the details
- [ ] I can always see in my mind's eye how to arrange furniture in a room, or pack a car boot in order to get everything in
- [ ] I have a sense of humour, which has at times got me into trouble
- [ ] I am good at ball and computer video games
- [ ] I loathe routine tasks.

___

Total right frontal

Left basal

- ☐ I don't like to have my routine disturbed
- ☐ I find filing, sorting and labelling relaxing
- ☐ I am uneasy with ambiguity and uncertainty
- ☐ I think rules are important and should be adhered to
- ☐ I always read the instruction leaflet before I use a new appliance
- ☐ If I have to do something tricky, I am happiest if I have an established protocol to follow
- ☐ I put my social commitments in my diary – and stick to them
- ☐ I have a place for everything – and everything is in its place
- ☐ I think people should keep their emotions under control
- ☐ I am reliable and loyal
- ☐ I enjoy doing repetitive tasks accurately
- ☐ I always tackle tasks step by step
- ☐ I like working with details
- ☐ I uphold traditional values
- ☐ I am reliable and thorough in my work.

___
Total left basal

Right basal

- [ ] My family and my relationships are the most important things in my life
- [ ] I automatically watch other people's faces when I am talking to them
- [ ] I know instinctively what people are thinking
- [ ] I feel uneasy when people start arguing around me
- [ ] I am good at making other people feel enthusiastic
- [ ] I think you can measure success by how happy you are feeling, rather than what you achieve
- [ ] I think spiritual values are more important than material things
- [ ] I often touch people spontaneously when I talk to them
- [ ] I am good at interpreting body language
- [ ] I cry easily at soppy films
- [ ] I think cooperation is the way to get things done, not conflict
- [ ] I tend to reach out to comfort people's body lagnuage
- [ ] I love to sing, dance and listen to music
- [ ] I think personal growth is something worth working at
- [ ] I think that feelings are more important than thoughts

Total right basal

2. When you have completed all the questions, count up the number of ticks in each section. Find the corresponding brain quadrant on the diagram below and place a dot on the number which matches your number of ticks.

3. Do this with each quadrant and then join up the dots. The kite shape indicates your individual brain map, showing which quadrants you use most.

If the balance is equal (about 5 percent of people), you have a strongly female brain.

Most people will use one quadrant strongly with supporting roles from two others. In this case, if the tendency is to the right you have a female brain; if it is predominantly to the left, you have a male brain. Men's brains tend to be more lopsided and rigidly compartmentalised than women's.

4. When you have created your brain map on the diagram, ask your partner or a friend to superimpose his or hers in a different coloured ink.

People often fall for someone whose brain map is similar to their own. But when it comes to forging a permanent relationship, we often seek those with very different brain maps, recognising that we need the input from the bits of brain that we rarely use.

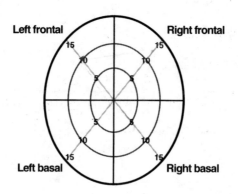

Find Out How You Think

How do you compare to these?

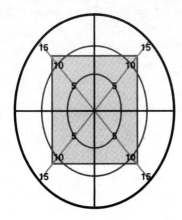

Well balanced and strongly female

Only 5 percent of people have a brain with such strength in all quadrants

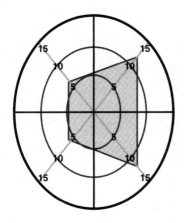

Typically female brain

Strength on the right side, in the areas dealing with creativity and emotions

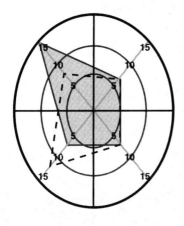

Typically male brain

Weak on emotions but powerful on logic and leadership. Very compartmentalised.

How it helps

Once you are aware of your thinking style and that of others you can help yourself and others to learn and to be more effective generally by approaching tasks and events in ways which are most acceptable to your brain.

Determine What You Value

What it is

Values are the things that are important to us; the things that underpin and influence our behaviour and the way we react. Their source is deep-seated and complex.

It is very hard to change values. It is therefore helpful to get in touch with your values and to understand the impact they have. This tool uses a simple questionnaire to help you rate your values.

How to use it

1. Assess each of the personal values listed on the next page on both scale A and scale B. Add the two to come up with an overall score.

2. Which of your top five values are being relatively well satisfied at present?

3. Which of your most important values are not being met?

4. What effect does this have on you and those around you?

5. Identify any ways that you can think of to change your current position to satisfy more of your values. You might like to discuss this with a friend, colleague or manager to get some ideas.

Rating scales

A	B
"How would you feel if your present satisfaction of this value was greatly reduced?"	"How would you feel if your present satisfaction of this value was greatly increased?"
1 = It wouldn't bother me 2 3 = Moderately concerned 4 5 = Devastated!	1 = It wouldn't matter 2 3 = Happy 4 5 = Terrific!
C = relative importance of the value to you (A + B)	

PERSONAL VALUES	C	=	A	+	B
Achievement (sense of accomplishment, mastery)					
Advancement (promotion)					
Adventure (new and challenging experiences)					
Affection (love, caring)					
Competitiveness (winning, taking risks)					
Cooperation (working well with others, teamwork)					
Creativity (being imaginative, innovative)					
Economic security (steady, adequate income)					
Fame (being famous, well known)					
Family happiness					
Freedom (independence, autonomy)					
Friendship (close relationships with others)					
Health (being physically and mentally well)					
Helpfulness (assisting others, improving society)					
Inner harmony (being at peace with yourself)					
Integrity (honesty, sincerity, standing up for beliefs)					
Involvement (participating with others, belonging)					
Loyalty (duty, respectfulness, obedience)					
Order (tranquillity, stability, conformity)					
Personal development (use of potential)					
Pleasure (fun, laughs, leisurely life-style)					
Power (control, authority, influence over others)					
Recognition (respect from others, status)					
Religion (strong religious beliefs)					
Responsibility (accountable for results)					
Self-respect (pride, sense of personal identify)					
Wealth (making money, getting rich)					
Wisdom (understanding life, discovering knowledge)					

List your five highest scoring values:

1 _____

2 _____

3 _____

4 _____

5 _____

How it helps

By being conscious of your values you can understand better your behaviour and the stress and frustrations you experience when your values are compromised. Once aware of them, you can choose to adjust your life so that your values and the way you spend your time are more attuned.

THE MORE YOUR LIFE IS IN TUNE WITH YOUR VALUES, THE LESS STRESS YOU WILL SUFFER

Be Clear What Drives You

What it is

People who own and manage their own careers are energised by motives which drive them. They take initiatives to increase the possibility of getting what they need and want from their lives, rather than passively reacting to things around them.

Career drivers are inner forces which determine what you want and need from your working life. Career drivers are not chosen consciously, but derive from your personality, abilities, values and self-image.

Awareness of your own career drivers will help you to do things which really suit you. Clarifying your drivers will help you to understand **what** you are looking for; not **how** to achieve it.

Drivers are not fixed; they do respond to changing circumstances. Security, for example, will become much more important with the arrival of a family.

Research shows that most people have two or three major drivers with only one at the core. It is the key driver that guides career progress and gives coherence to apparently unconnected choices and decisions.

This tool outlines the range of drivers (as developed by D Francis) and helps you to identify what drives you.

How to use it

1. Review the list of career drivers *(source : D Francis: Managing your own career)*. Each is a blend of wants and needs and although there is slight statistical overlap between some drivers you can think of them as being quite distinct.

The nine career drivers are:

- **Material rewards**
  - seeking possessions, wealth and a high standard of living. Having the trappings of wealth.

- **Power/influence**
  - seeking to be in control of people and resources. Having a significant leadership role. Being in charge.

- **Search for meaning**
  - seeking to do things which are believed to be valuable for their own sake, even though it may bring little tangible reward. Contributing to the wider community.

- **Expertise**
  - seeking a high level of accomplishment in a specialised field. Having a reputation as an expert.

- **Creativity**
  - seeking to innovate and be identified with original output. Doing something distinctively different.

- **Affiliation**
  - seeking meaningful, close relationships with others at work.

- **Autonomy**
  - seeking to be independent, able to make key decisions for yourself, managing your own time, being your own master.

- **Security**
  - seeking a solid and predictable future. Being financially secure. Taking the safe option.

- **Status**
  - seeking to be recognised, admired and respected by the community at large. Being seen as part of the 'establishment.'

2. Rank the drivers 1-9 to reflect how important you feel they are to you (1 = most important; 9 = least important)

3. Answer the following questions:

- how have the top two drivers influenced your life so far?

- how has your lack of concern for the bottom three drivers influenced your life so far?

- to what extent does your current role satisfy your career drivers?

- what are the implications of your drivers for your future?

How it helps

We are all driven by inner forces to meet our needs. This tool will help you to identify the nature of your personal drivers and to understand how well your current circumstances are in harmony with them.

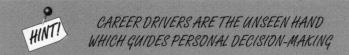

HINT!

CAREER DRIVERS ARE THE UNSEEN HAND
WHICH GUIDES PERSONAL DECISION-MAKING

Audit Your Skills

What it is

A skill is something you can do. It is easy to concentrate on what you can't do, or don't do very well. This tool gives you the opportunity to focus on what you're good at. Knowing your skills will increase your self-confidence and assertiveness and help you make the most of new opportunities.

How to use it

1. The first step is to stimulate your thoughts by making a list of a variety of experiences. The list can include:

- satisfying accomplishments/achievements at work

- participation in hobbies/sports

- voluntary or community work

- things you've done as a friend, parent, spouse, homeowner, etc

- the things that you are most proud of.

2. Search out any additional information you have on your skills. This data could include:

- competency profiles for you and for your job

- appraisal data

- customer feedback

- 360° feedback from peers, your team and your boss.

3. Use all this data to list:
   - your skills as a manager
   - your skills as a team-member
   - your skills as a technical expert (eg product development/ systems/finance/processing)
   - your skills in a project role.

4. Where possible, indicate to what standard you can perform these skills (eg are you an Olympic sprinter or a high school running champion?).

5. Now, review your answers to identify your key skills and interests, ie the things you're good at, like doing and want to develop further in the future.

Skills audit	Standards
Key management skills	
Key team-member skills	
Key technical skills	
Key project skills	
Others	

How it helps

By auditing your skills you will be more in touch with what you can do as a starting point for both self-development and career progression.

Describe Your Personality

What it is

Personality describes the behaviour and mental characteristics that make each of us unique. This tool does not include a full-blown personality assessment tool. Instead it offers a range of personality dimensions which you can use to paint a picture of yourself.

How to use it

1. Review the following scales. Plot where you feel you fall on each scale:

	Totally	Totally	
Are you intuitive			or analytical?
Are you extrovert			or introvert?
Are you a thinker			or a doer?
Are you creative and innovative			or prefer known routines?
Do you like detail			or prefer the overview?
Are you positive and 'sunny'			or serious and melancholy?
Do you like to lead			or be a follower?
Are you dogmatic			or easily influenced?
Are you full of energy and zest			or quiet and self-contained?
Do you feel more comfortable with black and white			or shades of grey?
Are you aggressive			or passive?
Do you express your feelings			or keep them to yourself?

2. Identify other words or phrases which describe your personality.

3. Ask someone else who knows you well to rate you against the scales and your own description (remember there is no right or wrong or good or bad profile). This will test the accuracy of your self-perception.

4. Reflect on the consequences of your personality:

- in what sort of role or situation are you likely to feel comfortable or ill at ease?

- what impact does your personality have on others?

- what sort of people do you get on with best?

- how can you counter what you may see as 'the downside' of your personality?

How it helps

Our personalities are fairly fixed. Short of a brain transplant they are hard to change. It is therefore important to be aware of the main features of our personalities and how they impact on others.

OTHERS OFTEN HAVE A MORE ACCURATE PERCEPTION OF YOUR PERSONALITY THAN YOU DO
SEEK FEEDBACK FROM PEOPLE YOU TRUST

2 Plan your life

Take a Process View

What it is

Career or life planning can be viewed as a process just like any other activity. This tool outlines the main steps in the process and the questions which must be answered.

How to use it

1. Review the process map on the next page.

2. Where are you on the map?

   - part-way through implementing a plan?

   - never thought about it?

   - achieved everything you ever wanted?

3. Are you happy with your position or do you want to move forward?

4. Identify which specific tools in this Toolbox you can use to help you.

How it helps

Life and career planning is a process; one that you both own and of which you are the prime customer. This tool outlines the main steps to help you clarify your current position.

The Life and Career Planning Process

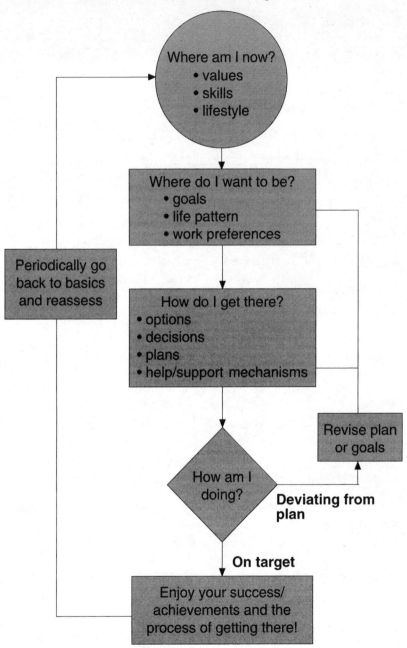

Where am I now?
- values
- skills
- lifestyle

Where do I want to be?
- goals
- life pattern
- work preferences

Periodically go back to basics and reassess

How do I get there?
- options
- decisions
- plans
- help/support mechanisms

Revise plan or goals

How am I doing?

Deviating from plan

On target

Enjoy your success/ achievements and the process of getting there!

Paint Your Future

What it is

This tool will help you paint a picture of what you want to become. Your vision of the future needs to be:

- based on realistic assumptions (about you and the circumstances in which you operate)
- in sufficient detail to be clear to you
- exciting and optimistic
- realistic (given your starting point!)
- grounded in your values and beliefs.

"Cheshire-Puss", Alice began, rather timidly, "would you tell me, please, which way I ought to go from here?"

"That depends a good deal on where you want to get to", said the Cat.

"I don't much care where ...," said Alice.

"Then it doesn't matter which way you go", said the Cat.

"... so long as I get somewhere", Alice added as an explanation.

"Oh, you're sure to do that", said the Cat, "If you only walk long enough".

Lewis Caroll,

Alice's Adventures in Wonderland

How to use it

1. Use the chart on the next page to build up a picture of how you would like your life to be in the next 2/3 years.

2. Identify up to five important areas of your life such as:

work	*education*
family	*interests/hobbies*
friends	*skills*
money	*religion*
health	*home*

3. Describe briefly the current reality.

4. Brainstorm how you would like each area to look in the future. Choose the number of years you feel is appropriate. What is your ideal vision of the future?

5. Review your vision of the future:

   - have you considered alternatives or just gone for your first idea?
   - does it feel good?
   - could you tell other people about it?
   - are you prepared to take action to achieve it?
   - does it fit with the way you like to live your life?
   - have you thought through the consequences?

6. Identify the key things which will have to change to achieve your vision.

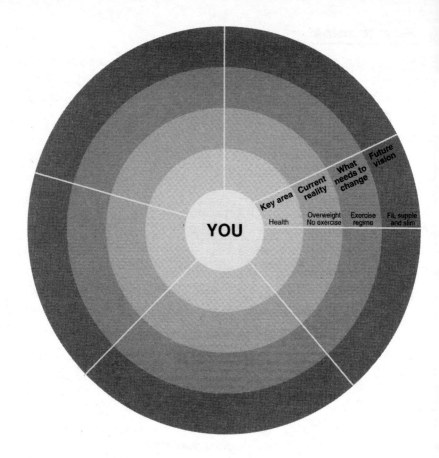

Key area | Current reality | What needs to change | Future vision

YOU

Health | Overweight No exercise | Exercise regime | Fit, supple and slim

7. In developing your career, it is helpful to:

- trust yourself, listen to your intuition on what to do

- keep yourself open to new experiences, be willing to respond to the moment and grasp opportunities

- be cautious about who you serve, be careful not always to neglect yourself for the benefit of others

- be authentic or honest with yourself and others. Games or pretence get in the way

- take care not to burn out, look after yourself

- enjoy the journey, not just the destination!

How it helps

This tool helps you simply to map out your vision for your life by describing both the future and the current reality. It will help you to find a balance between areas and to assess the size of the 'gap'.

or it may be more like this:

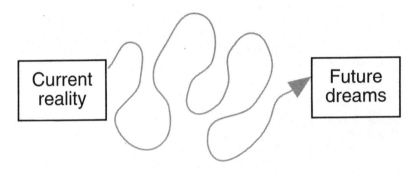

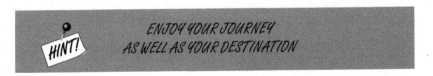

Define Your Goals

What it is

Once you have painted your vision of the future, the next step is to transform this broad insight into concrete objectives and then practical steps.

This tool gives you a mechanism for defining your goals and turning them into action.

How to use it

1. Take each 'dream' in your vision of the future.

2. Describe in one sentence how this is different to today's reality. Add a verb to turn it into a goal.

3. You have now defined what you want to achieve. You can now go on to define objectives which will be the means of achieving your goals. For example:

'Dream' area	Goal	Objectives
HEALTH	To be fit, supple and slim	• To lose 5 kg by the end of the year
		• To attend aerobics classes twice a week all year
		• To reduce my alcohol intake by 50% by midsummer

4. You are now ready to produce detailed action plans for each of the objectives you have identified for the next 12 months.

5. For each objective, complete the following action plan.

Objective

_____

_____

I will complete this objective by _____

It is important to me because _____

_____

These are the obstacles or restraining forces I may face and I will deal with them this way:

1. _____

2. _____

3. _____

These are the steps
I must take to reach
my goal: I must do it by:

1. _____   _____

2. _____   _____

3. _____   _____

4. _____   _____

How it helps

Dreams in themselves get you nowhere. It is the translation of these dreams into goals, objectives and actions that makes them real. This tool gives a simple method and pro formas for taking this essential step.

Make Choices

What it is

In life we regularly have to make choices such as whether to move jobs, get married, go on holiday or buy a car. These decisions can be time-consuming and energy sapping. This tool uses the simple method of Decision Charts to make life decisions.

How to use it

1. Identify the criteria which are important to you in the choice you have to make and insert in Column 1

   eg length of journey

   level of income

   location.

2. Rate the importance of the criteria and enter your score in Column 2

   0 = not important

   10 = absolutely crucial

3. Identify your options and show these in the remaining columns

   eg in terms of work:

   – *current job/project*

   – *next most likely job/project/assignment*

   – *most wanted job*

   – *dream job.*

4. For each option, assess the degree to which it meets your criteria

   0 = does not meet criteria

   10 = fully meets criteria

   and enter these in the top left hand corner of the relevant box.

5. Multiply the importance by the degree to which it is satisfied and enter this score in the bottom right hand corner of each box.

6. Calculate the total satisfaction for each option by totalling the figures in the bottom right hand corners. The option with the highest score is most likely to meet your requirements.

7. If you find yourself responding to the outcome with 'yes ... but' it suggests you have not articulated all the relevant criteria!

For example: evaluating job alternatives

Column 1	Column 2	Option 1	Option 2	Option 3	Option 4
Criteria	Importance of criteria	Sales Associate	Branch Manager	Regional Director	Professional Footballer
Economic security	10	4 / 40	6 / 60	8 / 80	5 / 50
Time with family	6	6 / 36	5 / 30	3 / 18	8 / 48
Total satisfaction					

How it helps

Failure to consider all the relevant factors is a common mistake in making decisions. This tool gives a simple method to help you decide between options.

Identify Your Development Needs

What it is

Once you are clear about your personal goals and objectives and you have audited your skills, this tool will help you to identify the additional knowledge, skills and experience you will need to achieve your goals.

How to use it

1. Review each of your personal goals.and objectives.

2. List out the knowledge, skills and experience you feel you will need to have to achieve the goal.

For example:

Goal	Knowledge needed	Skills needed	Experience needed
• To become a freelance travel writer	• Who's who in the travel business	• How to write articles for travel magazines	• Wide range of travel experiences in a variety of places
	• Expert knowledge of particular countries/ types of travel	• How to manage cashflow and business expenses	

3. Now decide which of these you feel you already have, ie you know you can do or you've had the experience. Tick these off.

4. Repeat this for each goal.

5. Develop a matrix of your unmet needs against your personal goals.

For example:

My develop-ment needs \ My personal goals	**1** To be a travel writer	**2** To own my own home	**3** To have a baby	**4** To learn French
To make contacts in the travel business	▲	○	○	■
To manage cash/flow and business expenses	▲	▲	▲	○
To broaden my travel experience	▲	■	■	■

▲ strong relationship   ■ some relationship   ○ no relationship

6. Identify those development needs which will make the greatest impact on all of your goals (remember this impact could be negative as well as positive).

7. Decide which needs are your top priority.

8. Develop an action plan to meet your needs.

9. Go do it!

How it helps

Meeting your development needs is both the means and the benefit of achieving your goals. This tool will help you to identify and prioritise your needs.

Overcome Resistance

What it is

It is worth spending a few minutes identifying the forces which you feel hold you back or act as barriers to your development. This tool uses Forcefield Analysis to help you identify these resistors and to plan how to tackle them.

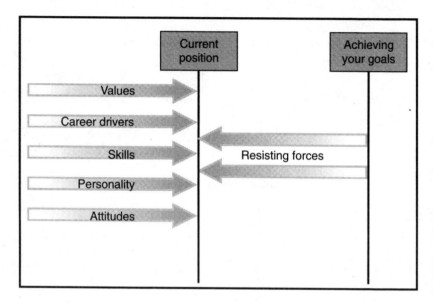

How to use it

1. Draw up a forcefield analysis diagram like the one above.

2. Earlier tools have helped you to identify all of the driving forces – your values, skills, personality and so on. Add these to your diagram.

3. Spend time identifying your resisting forces. Your resisting forces may be real or imaginary, and could be such things as:

   • health/gender/age

   • education

   • experience

- social class
- commitments
- location
- organisation, culture or structure

and perhaps, most important of all, your self-image.

Be honest with yourself. They must exist or you would be well on your way to achieving your goals by now.

. Identify which resistors are the strongest.

. Ask why? Why are they strong? Why are they there?

. Brainstorm everything you could do to remove, reduce or get around them.

. Identify an action you can take straight away to tackle the strongest resistor.

. Do it!

How it helps

There are times when we don't face up to issues or if we do, we don't take action to tackle them. Forcefield Analysis is a simple yet powerful tool to help you to identify your personal resistors (often self-inflicted) that are stopping you from achieving your goals.

'WE ARE WHAT WE THINK WE ARE'
SO GET IN TOUCH WITH WHAT YOU REALLY THINK!

3 Develop yourself

Use a Mentor

What it is

Mentoring is the occupational equivalent of a wise aunt or uncle who will act as a guide, supporter, counsellor and patron. During your career, several people will become your mentors. The trick is to find the best person to help you now.

Mentoring can be formally organised or left to occur 'naturally' as the need arises. This tool outlines how to find and use a mentor.

How to use it

1. Identify a potential mentor. A good mentor is likely to be someone:

   - who has the competencies you wish to develop

   - with wide experience and knowledge of the organisation (and therefore usually more senior than you)

   - working in an area you wish to move into too

   - with excellent coaching and development skills.

2. Approach the individual and explain what you are looking for and why s/he is such a good candidate. If they refuse, find an alternative.

3. Develop a contract which clarifies what you want. You need to agree:

   - what you both want to get out of the relationship

   - how you will work together, for example:
     - frequency of meetings
     - location
     - time available, etc.

- boundaries in terms of what you cover; access to information, etc
- how to monitor/review the value of your work together.

4. Diary dates ahead to avoid delays and frustration at a later stage.

5. Use your mentor to:
   - help you face reality and know your strengths and weaknesses
   - give feedback which is realistic and constructive
   - help you perceive or conceptualise in new ways by broadening your awareness and understanding
   - coach you in new competencies
   - make introductions and open doors
   - give guidance on career development
   - give specific advice and guidance on how to tackle things in your organisation
   - give personal support through change
   - share experience
   - build your confidence in your skills and abilities.

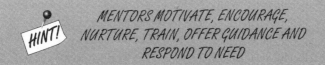

HINT!

MENTORS MOTIVATE, ENCOURAGE, NURTURE, TRAIN, OFFER GUIDANCE AND RESPOND TO NEED

How it helps

Using a mentor can increase your rate of development, improve your skills and broaden your awareness.

Build Your Network

What it is

Networking is the limitless process of talking to people for information, advice, contacts and even moral support.

This tool outlines how to build and use your network.

How to use it

1. Build your network

- Use every informal opportunity you can to meet people; conferences, meetings, social functions, trains, planes, etc.

- Join professional bodies and attend events.

- Keep in touch with former colleagues, friends and neighbours.

- Be prepared to take the initiative and introduce yourself.

- Always carry business cards and, if appropriate, add your home number.

- Don't be afraid to ask for business cards/numbers.

- Find out enough to know how and when a contact could be useful (job/company/location, etc).

- Be prepared to offer information to others, people are suspicious of one-way communication!

2. Maintain your network

- Develop a system for storing contact details. Make it easy to reference.

- Keep a note of relevant information about people.

- Keep your information up to date as people move, marry, have children, etc.

- Send Christmas cards, congratulations notes, anniversary cards, copies of articles, etc to keep in touch.

- Ring people from time to time to say hello, it's usually appreciated. Make a note of when you've done it.

- Invite contacts to social events, exhibitions, conferences, etc.

3. Use your network

- Call up contacts when you:

  - are searching for information

  - want an introduction or reference

  - need to know who to contact

  - are looking for potential customers

  - are job hunting.

- Always introduce yourself and if necessary remind your contact of where you met/spoke.

- Explain why you're making contact.

- Be clear what help or information you are seeking.

- Check if the time is appropriate or when would be better.

- Be polite, courteous and prepared to take 'no' for an answer.

- Acknowledge the help given.

- Offer to reciprocate when appropriate.

- Don't abuse, bombard or manipulate valuable contacts.

How it helps

Networking is a way of building informal contacts and links with others on a reciprocal basis. It can be a very useful source of information, advice and support. This tool outlines how to build, maintain and use your network.

Learn How to Learn

What it is

Learning is both a skill and a process. This tool builds on Kolb's learning cycle to give you practical tips on how to be a better learner.

How to use it

Kolb described effective learning as a four stage process:

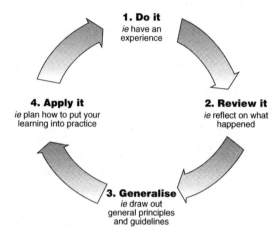

1. Do it
ie have an experience

2. Review it
ie reflect on what happened

3. Generalise
ie draw out general principles and guidelines

4. Apply it
ie plan how to put your learning into practice

1. Reflect on how you like to learn.

- Do you tend to sit back quietly and watch and listen?
- Are you hands on, always 'have a go' never mind the instructions?
- Are you always trying new ways of doing things?
- Do you feel comfortable with concepts and theories?
- Do you tend to repeat your mistakes?

2. It is likely that one or two stages of the cycle are much more comfortable and familiar to you than others. This is normal but can affect your ability to learn. Can you think of examples of this?

3. Use the following tips to improve your approach to each stage.

'Do it'

- Volunteer to get involved in new activities/projects/training/ conferences, etc or to sort out problems.

- Encourage your boss to delegate new work or let you substitute for her.

- Read new books, watch videos, play games, try new things and expose yourself to new experiences.

- Don't automatically say 'I can't .. I'm useless .. I'm too busy .. I'll make a mess of it', etc.

- Don't be afraid of getting it wrong, seek help and support if you're really concerned.

- See everything you do as a learning opportunity.

'Review it'

- After a new experience always step back and reflect on the detail:

  - who did what/who said what/who reacted

  - what went well/badly

  - what were the problems/successes etc.

- Seek feedback or observations from others on how you got on.

- Relive the experience in your mind to remember how it felt.

'Generalise'

- Step back from the detail in order to identify:

  - general patterns
  - do's and don'ts
  - principles, guidelines or checklists for future occasions.

- Summarise your 'learning points'.

'Apply it'

- Think through what you will do differently next time you are confronted with a similar task or problem.

- Be clear how you could be more effective or efficient; make notes or you will forget.

- Look for opportunities to 'have another go' quickly while your learning is still fresh.

How it helps

Real learning comes not just from doing but from reflecting on the experience, drawing out general learning points and thinking through how to apply them. This tool outlines practical ways in which you can do this.

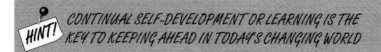

HINT! CONTINUAL SELF-DEVELOPMENT OR LEARNING IS THE KEY TO KEEPING AHEAD IN TODAY'S CHANGING WORLD

Increase Your Professionalism

What it is

Professionalism is about more than being paid to do a job or looking the part – it involves high standards of knowledge and skills; efficiency; integrity and no unnecessary hype. This tool defines these areas further and gives you some tips on how to put them into practice.

How to use it

1. Think about your role or job. When you talk of being professional, what specifically do you mean:

- qualifications?
- skills?
- reward?
- appearance?
- manner?
- other?

2. What specific standards are expected of you which would allow you to be judged as 'professional'?

3. Use this checklist to identify ways in which you could increase your professionalism:

Qualifications

✔ Have you passed the relevant exams for your work?

✔ Could you upgrade or update your qualifications?

✔ Do you belong to the relevant professional body?

✔ If so, do you meet their requirements for ongoing, professional development?

Skills

✔ Are you clear what skills or competencies are required for your work?

✔ Do you have all of these skills to the required standard? How do you know?

✔ Where are your shortfalls, the areas that go wrong or where you make mistakes?

✔ What can you do to polish or upgrade your skills?

Efficiency

✔ Do you do things accurately, completely and on time?

✔ Do you always deliver what you've promised, right first time or do you have a lot of re-work?

✔ Are you always rushing or cutting corners to meet deadlines?

Integrity

✔ Do you keep your promises?

✔ Do you honour confidences?

✔ Do you live by the standards you set for others?

✔ Do you give 'value for money' to your customers?

Appearance

✔ Do you dress appropriately for your role so you can perform your duties and remain safe, clean and tidy?

✔ Do you quietly get on with things or shout about it unnecessarily?

✔ Are you clear what your customers regard as acceptable?

Manner

✔ Do you appear calm and organised?

✔ Are you friendly without being too pally or intimate?

✔ Do you seem helpful and obliging?

✔ Do you build confidence in others by appearing confident (but not cocky) yourself?

IT IS FINE TO BE FLAMBOYANT, AS LONG AS SUBSTANCE MATCHES SHOW

4. If you have identified specific areas in which you can increase your professionalism – what are you going to do about them?

5. Spend some time developing an action plan. Try to find a way of seeking feedback or measuring the change so you will know if you have succeeded in upgrading your professionalism.

How it helps

In many ways, 'professionalism' is judged by your customer. There are many ways in which you can seek to improve their perception. This tool outlines the areas to tackle and helps you to assess where to start.

'PROFESSIONALISM' IS IN THE EYE OF YOUR CUSTOMERS. FIND OUT WHAT IT MEANS TO THEM

Take Empowerment

What it is

Empowerment is one of the buzz-words of the 90's and is often overused to suggest a general letting-go of authority. It is, in fact, a disciplined devolution of decision-making underpinned by both a clear framework of practical support and a value system that believes that everyone has more to offer and greater potential to fulfil if given the opportunity and appropriate environment. Empowerment is therefore about helping everyone to be of their best.

This tool uses a questionnaire to outline the practical framework that needs to be in place for empowerment to succeed. The key areas covered are:

- Goals and measures.
- Job and organisation design.
- Knowledge and skills.
- Management support.
- Recognition.

How to use it

1. Complete the following questionnaire focusing on your own position.
2. Consider giving a copy to your boss to get his views on your current level of empowerment.
3. Identify the areas you need to work on (the low scoring areas).
4. Develop an action plan to move forward.

For each of the questions listed below, please choose a response from the range:

4	Very satisfied
3	Satisfied
2	Slightly dissatisfied
1	Dissatisfied
0	Not applicable

Enter your response in the box against each question. Do not dwell on the questions, it should take no more than 15 minutes to complete them all. Only answer 'very satisfied' if all parts of the question are true.

How satisfied are you that........

1. You have very stretching, clear targets to achieve.

2. You feel part of a team/have a sense of belonging/loyalty.

3. You are able to get appropriate education and training to develop yourself and are encouraged and supported to do so.

4. You are thanked personally for a job well done (by your customers/suppliers/managers/peers).

5. Your manager regularly reviews your training needs with you and takes action as a result.

6. You are involved in setting your targets.

7. You have sufficient contact with your customers and receive useful feedback and data on requirements.

8. You are encouraged to come up with improvements and to take appropriate action as a result. ☐

9. You have measures that tell you how well you are doing and you use them to identify improvements. ☐

10. Team as well as individual achievements are recognised. ☐

11. You can speak up about your mistakes and this is received constructively. ☐

12. You are encouraged to challenge the status quo and your manager listens generously to your views and ideas. ☐

13. You are able to make day-to-day decisions about your work to meet your customers' needs and are encouraged to do so. ☐

14. You understand how achieving your targets will contribute to the overall goals of the company. ☐

15. You receive feedback from your customers (internal and external) on your performance without asking. ☐

16. You are asked to input to future team plans and strategies. ☐

17. You feel appropriately recognised for your achievements. ☐

18. You have all the right knowledge and skills to do your job. ☐

19. You feel able to speak to your manager about problems and concerns and this is really listened to. ☐

20. Your manager praises you when you do well and gives you constructive feedback on areas for improvement. ☐

21. You have all the resources you need to do your job (eg equipment, materials). ☐

22. You receive active help and encouragement from your manager to improve your knowledge and skills. ☐

23. Your manager understands your values and ambitions and takes steps to help you fulfil them. ☐

24. You are clear about the limits of your decision-making authority. ☐

25. When necessary, you can take decisions which exceed your normal authority without reference to your manager (provided you can justify your actions). ☐

Your responses can usefully be represented under five dimensions:

The total scores for each dimension can then be shown on a chart and comparisons made between team members:

Job design	Knowledge & skills	Goals & Measures	Management support	Recognition & reward
2 ☐	3 ☐	1 ☐	12 ☐	4 ☐
7 ☐	5 ☐	6 ☐	19 ☐	10 ☐
13 ☐	8 ☐	9 ☐	22 ☐	15 ☐
21 ☐	11 ☐	14 ☐	23 ☐	17 ☐
24 ☐	18 ☐	16 ☐	25 ☐	20 ☐

Totals:

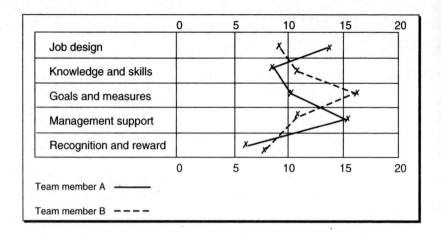

	0	5	10	15	20
Job design					
Knowledge and skills					
Goals and measures					
Management support					
Recognition and reward					

Team member A ———

Team member B – – – –

How it helps

Increasing your empowerment will help you develop your skills, make your job more satisfying and broaden your experience.

DON'T WAIT FOR SOMEONE ELSE TO
GIVE IT TO YOU;
IDENTIFY WHAT YOU CAN DO TO
BECOME EMPOWERED

Measure Yourself

What it is

Measurement is a vital tool on the road to self-improvement. Just as it is helpful to know your weight if you're trying to diet, or your handicap if you play golf, so it is useful to know how you're doing against work objectives or specific competencies. This tool outlines the range of measures you can use and gives some tips on how to set them up.

How to use it

1. Identify the main aspects of your life. For example:

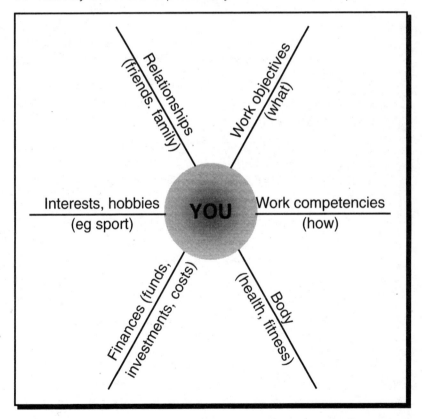

2. For each aspect, identify the measures (if any) that you currently have to track how you're doing. Add these to the diagram.

For example:

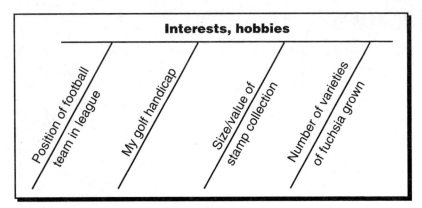

Interests, hobbies

Position of football team in league

My golf handicap

Size/value of stamp collection

Number of varieties of fuchsia grown

3. Review your chart.

- Are there areas of your life where you have no measures? (however 'soft' and subjective). Do you want to add any?

- Are there areas where you have too many and maybe you're trying to do too much and not achieving a great deal? Do you want to remove any?

- Are your measures as SMART as they might be? (ie Specific, Measurable, Achievable, Realistic and Timebound). If not, can you make them so?

- Are you satisfied with your current performance against all of your measures? If not, which do you need to work on? What do you need to do?

4. Amend your chart to show the measures you feel will be most appropriate and useful to you. Identify and add targets.

5. Review your chart regularly to check your progress.

How it helps

Articulating the measures you use on yourself will help you to check the balance in your life; identify areas where you need to improve and give your feedback on progress. This tool gives a simple method for doing this.

Develop a Positive Self-image

What it is

Our self-image is based on our experiences and perceptions of ourselves. It can be either positive or negative. It influences the way we behave and how we feel about ourselves. This tool will help you get in touch with your self-image and help you take steps to be more positive.

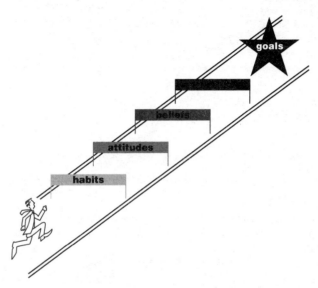

How to use it

1. Review the self-made hurdles to your success.

- What habits, attitudes, beliefs and expectations do you have that act as hurdles to reaching your goals?

- What statements do you regularly use to describe yourself? Which of these are negative?

  - *"We've always done it that way ..."*

  - *"We're too busy ..."*

  - *"Women can't do that ..."*

  - *"It'll never work ..."*

  Write them down. Look at how limiting they can be.

- Do you base your decisions only on past experience? Are you limiting your potential by assuming the future will be like the past?

- What situations do you avoid because you find them uncomfortable? When do you stay inside your comfort zone? What boundaries do you place around yourself?

- What do you do because you 'have to' as opposed to 'want to'?

- What are the 'stones in your shoes' (the things that niggle or hurt and stop you moving as far or as fast as you might)?

- What sort of messages or tapes play inside your head?

  I'm good ... I'm loved ... I'm growing ...

  or

  I can't do that ... Nobody likes me ... I'm tired ...

  How does this self-image influence your current performance?

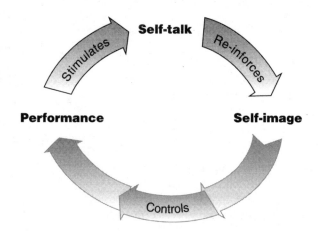

Develop a Positive Self-image

2. Take steps to improve your self-image.

- Develop your goals, be positive and consistent. Remind yourself of them daily. Tell others who can help you achieve them. Keep imagining what it will be like when you have succeeded. Focus on what you want to achieve. Be a self starter!

- Reprogramme your self-image by making regular 'affirmations' to yourself

  - imagine what specific successes will look like

  - turn the future into statements in the present tense:

  - *"I am a good tennis player"*

  - "I can make difficult decisions"

  - *"I really enjoy public speaking"*.
  Repeat these statements to yourself, daily. As you say the words, visualise the picture and feel the emotion.

- Give yourself positive feedback when things go well

  - "... good job ... I did that really well."

  - *"... a real improvement ... congratulations!"*

Listen when others give you praise and believe it, don't just hear the criticism. Build a positive picture of yourself.

- Work on extending your comfort zone; look for opportunities; seek support and help from others, take small, short steps until you get used to it; believe it will be OK!

- Look for solutions, don't wallow in problems or excuses. Have a 'can do ...' approach. Keep focused on the benefits of achieving success.

- Take ownership and responsibility for things. Don't pass the buck or wait for others. Believe you can make the difference.

How it helps

Our self-image is one of the most important influences on our behaviour and our success. This tool gives some practical steps to get in touch with your self-image as it is today and some tips on how to improve it for tomorrow.

4 Get organised

Focus on Your Goals
What it is

Managing time means addressing the need to be effective (doing the right things) as well as efficient (doing things right). This tool gives you a process for focusing on your goals, which is the first step in improving your time management.

 HINT! *AGREE CLEAR GOALS AND OBJECTIVES*

How to use it

1. Work with your boss to identify your key result areas, eg sales levels/budget performance/productivity.

2. Identify specific objectives and targets for the next year/quarter/month. The timescale will vary with the type and level of job you do.

3. Devise appropriate measures to track your performance.

4. Ensure that your goals and targets are aligned with the departmental/organisational goals and reflect your customer requirements.

5. Set review dates through the year.

6. Complete the following proforma to record your objectives, etc and to review your progress.

7. Agree your priorities between objectives. Consult your boss, your customers and your suppliers as necessary.

Key Result Area 1					
Objectives	Measures	Targets	Deadlines	Review date	Priority ranking

Key Result Area 2					
Objectives	Measures	Targets	Deadlines	Review date	Priority ranking

8. Plan your time.

- For each objective, identify the activities or tasks to be done.

- Develop 'to do' lists – daily/weekly/monthly and project plans.

- Use your diary to plan your day/week/month. Book time for:
  - project work
  - meetings
  - reading
  - visiting customers.

- Identify a daily routine which suits you and your customers.

9. Make your plans happen!

10. Regularly review your progress and success.

How it helps

Keeping your eyes and your time focused on what you have to achieve will help you to get results. This tool gives you practical steps to help you do this.

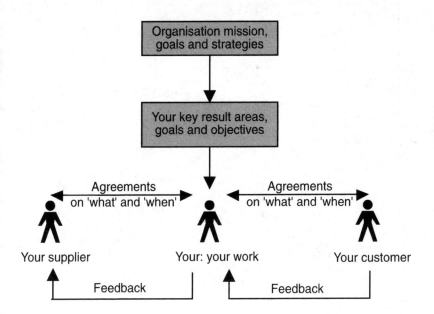

Define Your Priorities

What it is

It is important to set priorities so that the most important and urgent tasks get done first. This tool gives you an effective mechanism for doing this.

How to use it

1. Decide the priority of an activity in terms of its importance (ie its contribution to your overall success or achievement of an objective) and its urgency (ie how soon you have to do it).

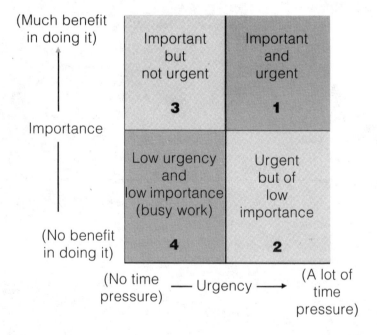

2. Use this framework to decide the priority of a task. You can do it on a piece of paper but a large wall chart and coloured Post-Its® will keep it visible.

3. Plan to do the important and urgent tasks first. Fit the urgent but not important tasks in quickly after this and put time aside when you will do the important but not urgent things. In addition, identify time-wasters which are neither urgent not important, and resolve to ignore them.

4. The Pareto principle usually applies to time – 80% of your results are probably generated in 20% of your time. Keep your eye on the vital 'few'.

5. Continually re-evaluate your activities in the light of your goals and priorities and adjust your grid.

How it helps

Setting priorities on the basis of agreed goals and using them to determine what gets your time will really increase your effectiveness. This grid will help you to organise your time.

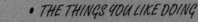

WATCH OUT FOR SETTING PRIORITIES ON THE BASIS OF:
- THE THINGS YOU LIKE DOING
- THE THINGS YOU KNOW HOW TO DO BEST
- THE THINGS THAT ARE EASIEST
- THINGS IN THEIR ORDER OF ARRIVAL
- WHOEVER SHOUTS LOUDEST
- HITTING DEADLINES AT THE LAST MINUTE

HINT!

Plan Your Time

What it is

Planning is a key to success. This tool gives you a checklist on how to plan and organise your time.

How to use it

1. Use the time management funnel to plan how to use your time.

2. Review this checklist and identify how to improve your use of time:

Agree goals and objectives

Set priorities

Identify 'to dos': what/who/when/how

Use your personal diary
to plan each
Day/week/month/year

Ask: What is the most
effective use of my
time right now?

✔ Schedule your time to ensure that you accomplish the most important things first

✔ Leave buffer time between scheduled tasks to allow for the unexpected and for interruptions. Have a list of activities that you could be working on during buffer time

✔ Make sure the first hour of your working day is productive. This sets the theme for the rest of the day

✔ Arrange for at least one period a day eg $1/2$ hour or 1 hour, when you are free from interruptions so you can tackle your important thinking tasks

✔ Take breaks when possible at times when you cannot work or think effectively

✔ Do tasks which require maximum thinking capacity when you are at your best

✔ Make sure that, each day, you do some work on a major goal. Do not just fill the day with maintenance activities

✔ Do one task at a time

✔ Do not procrastinate. If it is too big and daunting, break it down into manageable bits. If it is unpleasant, develop the killer instinct; do it first thing in the morning

✔ Make sure you build in time for yourself to relax, eg some exercise such as walking. It helps you regain the overview, lengthens your 'prime time' (when you are working well) and reduces the 'troughs'

 HINT!   FAILING TO PLAN IS PLANNING TO FAIL

3. Decide how much time to spend on an activity.

- Think in terms of the time-benefit ratio: how much time it is worth spending on the activity considering its value.

- Use the law of diminishing returns. With many activities, the benefits reduce as you spend more time on them. Consider whether you could invest this extra time more profitably in another, higher payoff, activity.

- Set time limits and deadlines for all tasks you do. This can range from formal deadlines to a quick, on- the spot, estimation of how long the tasks will take and by when you should finish.

- Develop the habit of finishing what you start. Do not jump from one thing to another leaving several unfinished tasks behind you.

- Take the time to do it right first time. You will not have to waste time later doing it over again.

- Delegate if you can. It gives you more time to think and manage and helps you achieve much more as well as developing your staff.

DELEGATION ALLOWS YOU TO FOCUS ON YOUR TOP PRIORITIES

How it helps

It is not always possible to plan. You will be hit with ad hoc requests, problems to sort out, other people's priorities to meet and so on. However, most people can control some of their time. Use this tool to help you get the most out of this precious resource.

Use Time Planners

What it is

There is a range of time tools available to help you organise your time. These can all be either paper based or electronic. Used well, they can save you a great deal of time and wasted effort.

How to use it

1. Review the following tools and decide which is most appropriate for you.

✔ **Diary:**
- use to plan ahead
- allocate time for your customers, your team, your suppliers and yourself
- note review/reminder dates

YOU HAVE TO SPEND TIME TO SAVE TIME; BUT THE RETURN ON YOUR INVESTMENT CAN BE HUGE!

✔ **Daily planner - each day note:**
- results to achieve
- actions to take
- people to speak to
- meetings to attend

✔ **Weekly/monthly planner:**
- set short-term goals
- plan out the week/month, leaving space for contingencies

✔ Wall charts:

- make target dates visible to everyone, use them to coordinate team plans

✔ Speak to charts:

- make a note of things to speak to individuals about

- only call/visit when you have accumulated several things (if they are minor)

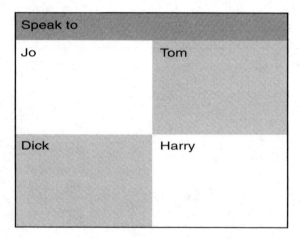

✔ To do lists:

- note things to do as and when they occur

- decide when to do things if at all possible and enter in your diary/charts on the approprate date

✔ Bring forward files:

- set up a filing drawer with one file for each month, ie 1-12 and one for each day of one month, ie 1-31. Place progress files in the file corresponding to the day or month you next expect to have to deal with them or to remind you to deal with them. *Throw away your pending tray!*

✔ **Voice Mail/E-mail:**

- if you have access to these systems use them to answer queries/brief others/seek information. They can save a huge amount of chasing and 'telephone tag'

- beware, however, of never speaking directly to others. Your relationships can suffer

---

2. Get yourself equipped with the right materials.

3. Have a go for a month; experiment; don't give up if at first it seems time-consuming; you'll get faster.

4. At the end of the month, review how it has gone - what has helped and in what ways; what doesn't work for you.

5. Adjust your approach and trial it again for another month.

6. Keep on 'doing and reviewing' until you have the ideal toolkit for you.

How it helps

Tools are only as good as their master. The correct range of time tools, used well, will really help you get organised and in control of your time.

 AIM TO BE THE MASTER OF YOUR TIME; NOT ITS SLAVE

Remove Time Wasters

What it is

It is easy to fritter away time if you're not careful. This tool will help you to understand where your time goes and gives you some practical tips on removing time-wasters.

How to use it

1. You need to start by understanding how you use your time now. Use the following proforma to record how you spend your time on, say, three typical working days.

 KEEPING A LOG CAN SEEM A REAL PAIN, BUT IT IS WORTH IT; YOU CAN'T IMPROVE UNTIL YOU UNDERSTAND THE PROBLEM

TIME LOG: _____   **DATE:** _____

At each checkpoint, simply tick the dominant activity of the last 15 minutes.

Time	Phone	Pre-planned meeting	Project work	Daily routine work	Post (in-tray)	Interruptions	Social	Other
8.00								
8.15								
8.30								
8.45								
9.00								
9.15								
9.30								
9.45								
10.00								
10.15								
10.30								
10.45								
11.00								
11.15								
11.30								
11.45								
12.00								
12.15								
12.30								
12.45								
1.00								
1.15								
1.30								
1.45								
2.00								
2.15								
2.30								
2.45								
3.00								
3.15								
3.30								
3.45								
4.00								
4.15								
4.30								
4.45								
5.00								
5.15								
5.30								
5.45								
6.00								

2. At the end of the three days, summarise the results:

Time	Day 1	Day 2	Day 3	Average	% time
On phone					
In pre-planned meetings					
Project work					
Daily routine work					
Dealing with in-tray					
Handling interruptions					
Socialising					
Other (please specify)					
					100%

3. Now that you know how you spend your time, use the other tools in this section of the Toolbox to help you focus on your goals and priorities and plan your time.

4. There will still be things that 'get in the way'. Here are some tips for handling time wasters:

    - Identify the root causes of wasted time.

    - Avoid blaming others, take responsibility.

    - If you cannot remove it, identify ways of minimising the impact.

MAKE REMOVING TIME WASTERS A REGULAR DISCIPLINE

- If staff are continually checking with you or seeking your approval – delegate more.

- Discourage others from keeping you informed at too detailed a level.

- Anticipate what information staff will need and give it in team meetings or memos.

- Be more self disciplined about socialising. Save small talk for breaks, unless it is intentionally for relationship building.

BE HONEST WITH YOURSELF ON HOW YOU WASTE TIME

- Talk to constant interrupters – let them know when you are available and when you prefer not to be interrupted.

- Do not regard the open door policy as meaning you need to be available all the time to all people.

- Be discriminating. Identify the key people who need access to you all the time.

- If you have a secretary, let him/her deal with the rest, or if you do not have one, take control of the interruption.

- If you are interrupted: check what the interrupter wants; weigh up whether you can deal with it now (ie how important and urgent is it compared with what you are working on at the moment).

5. Learn how to say no: if you do not know how to refuse requests, you become governed by other people's priorities and unable to achieve your own priorities, ie

- Check out what the request is, resist your first impulse, eg "of course I will" or "no, I can't"; ask for clarification or more information.

- Choose an appropriate way of saying no ... "sorry, I can't" ... but always say what you can do to help "I'm unable to today but I can spend two hours on it tomorrow" or explore alternatives "I'm unable to but let's see who else could".

> *BEWARE OF BEING GOVERNED*
> *BY OTHER PEOPLE'S PRIORITIES*

6. After say three months, repeat the time log exercise to measure whether or not you have improved your use of time.

> *BE RUTHLESS WITH TIME,*
> *GRACIOUS WITH PEOPLE*

How it helps

If you want to solve a problem you need to understand what it is. Time is precious – manage it, don't squander it.

5 Work well with others

Be Assertive

What it is

There are three ways of interacting with others – aggressively, assertively or non–assertively (passive). Each is described by typical verbal or behavioural patterns.

Assertive behaviour is most likely to achieve success in the long term as it encourages win–win results.

This tool describes the three types of behaviour and outlines a process for improving your assertiveness.

How to use it

1. Examine your general behaviour

How do you generally behave? (This can be affected by your general mood, your feeling of well being, who you have to work with, level of work pressure, etc.)

Are you being assertive or non-assertive or aggressive at work at present? (See checklist for typical behaviours.)

Decide whether there are underlying negative influences that are throwing you off balance.

Typical verbal and non-verbal signals of behaviour

VERBAL	NON–VERBAL
ASSERTIVE	**ASSERTIVE**
• Makes statements that are clear, brief and to the point. • Distinguishes between fact and opinion. • Uses firm voice and clear speech. • When critical is constructive, without blaming. • Questions to find out thoughts, opinions, wants of others. • Looks for ways of solving problems.	• Key words emphasised. • Smiles when pleased, frowns when angry. • Steady features. • Open hand movements. • Alert posture.
NON–ASSERTIVE	**NON–ASSERTIVE**
• Makes long rambling statements. • Uses fill-in words, such as 'perhaps'. • Offers apologies, and asks for permission. • Voice is dull, flat, whining. • Uses phrases that dismiss own needs (eg "It's not important really") • Self–critical (eg "I'm no good at this…").	• Hesitant manner. • Clears throat frequently. • Nervous smile when expressing anger. • Avoids eye contact. • Arms crossed. • Defensive posture.
AGGRESSIVE	**AGGRESSIVE**
• Expresses opinions as facts. • Uses threatening questions. • Requests are expressed as instructions or threats. • Voice is sharp or shouting. • Blames others. • Makes assumptions. • Uses sarcasm and makes negative remarks about others.	• Facial expressions distant, cold. • Scowls when angry. • Jaws set firm. • Trys to stare down, dominate. • Points finger, bangs fist. • Walks round impatiently. • Uses threatening posture.

2. Review how you respond to particular situations

You may be less assertive in some situations than in others. There may be situations you try to avoid, in order to avoid the need to act assertively. You could keep a record at work for a period of a week, of situations in which you did not behave assertively, why you think you did not and how you could tackle a similar situation differently in the future.

Situation	How I behaved	How I wish I had behaved	Why the difference?

3. Analyse particular situations

Take a few moments to review how you handled the situations where you found it difficult to be assertive. Consider both your verbal and your nonverbal behaviour.

4. Consider alternative responses

Identify other options you could adopt in the future to handle yourself, to handle the other people involved and to bring each situation to a successful conclusion.

Watch out for the way other people handle similar situations – can you learn from what they do?

When you have identified situations in which you need to be more assertive, these guidelines may help you move towards more effective behaviour.

5. Try out alternative responses

Try out new ways of behaving in situations that cause you problems. Check the effect of your 'new' behaviour on the results you achieve, and on the other people involved.

6. Trust yourself and your feelings

An assertive person is open and direct. Tell people how you feel, and what you want and need. Get to the point Volunteer information and initiate conversations.

7. Be clear and keep to the point

Keep to the issue at hand. Be a problem solver rather than a problem raiser, in order to achieve positive results. Separate feelings from facts in what you say, and in evaluating what others say. Act on your convictions.

8. Confront issues

Don't accept 'put downs' or disregard yourself. Be willing to disagree. Confront issues in a straightforward manner. If you are seen to be assertive, you lessen the likelihood that others will try to use or manipulate you. You will gain the respect of others, as well as building your own self respect.

9. Reduce aggression

If your need is to reduce your aggressiveness you can:

- ask for opinions of others
- negotiate decision making
- listen without interrupting
- adapt to the true needs of others
- allow others to assume leadership more often.

How it helps

By acting assertively you are more likely to ensure that your views, ideas and feelings are considered when changes are to be made. It is also more likely that you will take into account the views of others when instigating improvements, so increasing the chance of success.

 BEING ASSERTIVE HELPS EVERYBODY FEEL MORE OK ABOUT THEMSELVES

Listen Actively

What it is

Listening Actively means listening beyond just the words, to obtain their real meaning.

How to use it

1. Quieten your own mind

- Put aside other matters and concerns.
- Do not interrupt.
- Do not finish other people's sentences.
- Breathe calmly and deeply.

2. Control the environment

- Shut out background noise as much as possible.
- Stop interruptions.
- Remove physical barriers.
- Get fairly close to the speaker.
- Don't invade their personal space.

3. Listen carefully to what is being said

- Focus on the speaker.
- Shut out your thoughts and reactions.
- Give the speaker your full, unbiased attention.

4. Use positive nonverbal signals

- Nodding.
- Smiling.
- Attentive posture.
- Interested facial expression.
- Eye contact.

5. Use positive verbal signals

- "Ah ah".
- "Good idea".
- "I like that".
- "I hadn't thought of that before".

- "Interesting".
- Prompting (repeating the speaker's most significant words or phrases).

6. Use pauses

- Spaces are natural.
- Don't try and fill the silence.
- Allow time for absorption and reflection.
- Don't rush or hurry the speaker unnecessarily.
- Relax.

7. Summarise

Restate your understanding of the content and/or reflect feelings.

- "Let me check to make sure I understood ..."
- "You're saying that .."
- "As I understand you ..."
- "Let me see if I've got that. The goal for this session is ..".

8. Avoid unhelpful behaviours

- Don't doodle.
- Don't stare or look aggressive.
- Don't hide behind a barrier.
- Don't keep looking at your watch.

How it helps

Listening Actively ensures you really focus on the other person's views, ideas and feelings and helps to ensure true two-way communication.

YOU HAVE TWO EARS AND ONE MOUTH — USE THEM IN THOSE PROPORTIONS

Ask Questions

What it is

Questions are used to draw out information from others.

How to use it

There are several types of questions. Choose the most appropriate:

1. Open-ended questions

Open questions promote discovery and stimulate thinking. They are useful to help the other person start talking about a topic, outline a situation, give a broad description of what happened and how he or she reacted.

There are three broad types of open question:

- **Clarifying questions**

  - "What specifically does that mean to you?"

  - "Can I make sure I understand that ...?"

  - "If I hear correctly, what you are saying is ..."

- **Creative questions**

  - "How have you seen others handle similar situations?"

  - "What do you think about...?"

  - "Would you like to talk more about it?"

  - "I'd be interested in hearing more"

  - "What would be your approach if there were no constraints?"

- **Process questions**

  - "What would you like to get from this session?"

  - "What do I need to communicate to ensure everyone understands your role?"

  - "What authority do you think you need to complete this task?"

2. Follow-up or probing questions

The purpose of follow-up questions is to get information, broaden decisions and understand reasons and motivations. Do not over use 'why'. It causes people to become defensive.

- "In what way would this help achieve greater customer satisfaction?"

- "What other aspects of this should be considered?"

- "How would you involve others in accomplishing this plan?"

Follow-up questions are useful for probing – getting to the heart of a topic, checking information and filling in detail.

A particular type of follow-up question is the reflective question, useful for gaining a clearer understanding, revealing more information or uncovering feelings.

- "You say you were pleased..."

- "You seem to feel angry about this...?"

- "You say he reacted to this. How did he react...?"

3. Closed questions

Closed questions are those that lead to either 'yes' or 'no'. They are useful in checking facts quickly but canlead to a one-sided conversation. Examples are:

- "Have you been shopping recently?"

- "Is there enough money in the bank?"

- "Have you done this sort of work before?"

A closed question can be a useful lead into open questions once an area to explore has been identified.

4. Less useful questions

Certain types of questions are less useful. Try not to use them – these include:

- leading questions ("I assume you...")
- hypothetical questions ("If you were in my place...")
- multiple questions.

I HAVE SIX GOOD FRIENDS AND TRUE,
THEY TAUGHT ME ALL I KNEW.
THEIR NAMES ARE WHAT AND WHEN AND HOW
AND WHY AND WHERE AND WHO R KIPLING

5. The questioning funnel

Questions can be most effective when used in series to gather information. The funnel Illustrates how:

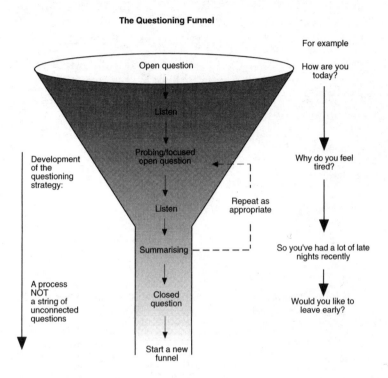

The Questioning Funnel

For example

Open question — How are you today?

Listen

Development of the questioning strategy:

Probing/focused open question — Why do you feel tired?

Listen

Repeat as appropriate

Summarising — So you've had a lot of late nights recently

A process NOT a string of unconnected questions

Closed question — Would you like to leave early?

Start a new funnel

How it helps

Questions are the only way to seek information and to fully involve an individual. Along with listening they ensure two-way communication.

Aim for Win-Win

What it is

Win-win is the optimum solution to problems or conflict. It means that you feel that you have got what you wanted but so do the others involved because you have built on each others ideas and views to produce the optimum outcome.

Win-win avoids put downs, mediocre compromises or 'either – or' and increases the chance of full buy-in to actions. This tool will help you assess your approach to conflict situations as a starting point for being more 'win-win'.

How to use it

1. Review the Thomas Kilman model of conflict-handling styles:

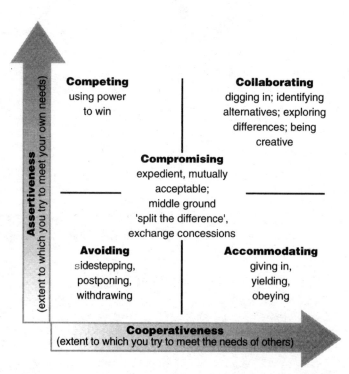

Each of us will tend to use one or two of these styles when faced with a conflict situation.

2. Use the following questions to help you identify your predominant style. Only answer yes if you regularly behave in this way – BE HONEST!

	Yes	No
• Competing		
Are you firm in pursuing your goals?	☐	☐
Do you always try to win?	☐	☐
Do you put effort into getting your own way?	☐	☐
Do you press to make your point?	☐	☐
Do you sell hard the benefits of your idea?	☐	☐
Are you surrounded by yes-men?	☐	☐
• Collaborating		
Do you try to deal with everyone's concerns?	☐	☐
Do you seek others' help in working out solutions?	☐	☐
Do you try and get everyone's concerns out on the table?	☐	☐
Do you express your views and encourage others to do the same?	☐	☐
Do you try and work openly through differences?	☐	☐
Are you concerned with meeting everyone's needs?	☐	☐
• Compromising		
Do you try to find a compromise solution?	☐	☐
Do you give up some points in exchange for others?	☐	☐
Do you propose 'the middle ground'?	☐	☐
Do you try and balance gains and losses?	☐	☐

- **Avoiding**

    Do you let others take responsibility for solving problems? □ □

    Do you try to avoid tension or controversy? □ □

    Do you try to avoid creating 'unpleasantness'? □ □

    Do you postpone issues 'to think it over'? □ □

- **Accommodating**

    Do you focus on areas of agreement rather than difference? □ □

    Do you try to soothe feelings to preserve relationships? □ □

    Do you often sacrifice your own wishes? □ □

    Do you avoid hurting others' feelings by disagreeing

3. Once you have identified your predominant style(s) then ask yourself:

    - is my style always appropriate?

    - if not, why not? What are the disadvantages?

    - do you 'overplay' your style; being too competitive/too accommodating, etc? What are the consequences?

    - what can you do to improve your flexibility of style?

How it helps

Conflict handling is an important skill when building relationships. This tool helps you identify your typical approach to conflict situations and gives you ideas on the behaviours you need to work on to increase your adaptability. By choosing the right style for particular situations you increase the chances of a win-win outcome.

Consult Effectively

What it is

Many people have to influence and support change without any authority over the resources involved. While they may be technical experts in finance, HR, law, systems, etc, they can struggle to fulfil their roles as internal consultants simply through a lack of an operating process or method. This tool outlines a seven step process which can significantly increase the effectiveness of 'experts'.

How to use it

1. Review the seven step process for effective consulting.

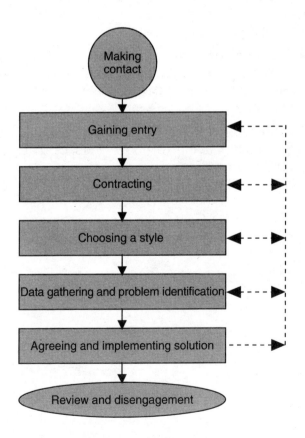

The seven steps involve:

Step 1: making contact – getting in touch with a potential client and arranging to meet.

Step 2: gaining entry – establishing sufficient mutual trust to proceed. This involves sharing histories, experiences and views to build comfort levels and rapport.

Step 3: contracting – agreeing what is to be achieved; boundaries; resources; timescales; operating methods; responsibilities, etc.

Step 4: choosing a style – deciding whether to simply follow the client's lead and directions; take control of the assignment or collaborate in a joint problem-solving process.

Step 5: data gathering and problem identification – using a range of tools and methods to gather information, analyse and get to key issues and root causes.

Step 6: agreeing and implementing solution – identifying, exploring and getting agreement to the best way forward. Developing plans and coordinating and taking action to make it happen.

Step 7: review and disengagement – evaluating results and learning points. Clearing up loose ends. Updating records and ensuring a clean break.

2. Consider how (or if) you apply these steps.

3. How effective are you at each step.

4. What goes well? What do you find difficult?

5. Identify steps you can take to improve your effectiveness.

6. Try them out and review their effect.

7. Identify further improvements.

How it helps

This tool outlines a seven step process or methodology to help an 'expert' use their expertise to bring about change, where they have no authority over the resources involved. Coupled with effective interpersonal skills, it provides a simple recipe for effective consultancy.

Adapt Your Style

What it is

The situational leadership model developed by Hersey and Blanchard is one of the most widely accepted frameworks for describing and improving management behaviour. This tool outlines the model, helps you to identify your typical style and gives you some thought starters on matching your style to the situation.

How to use it

1. Review the Hersey and Blanchard model:

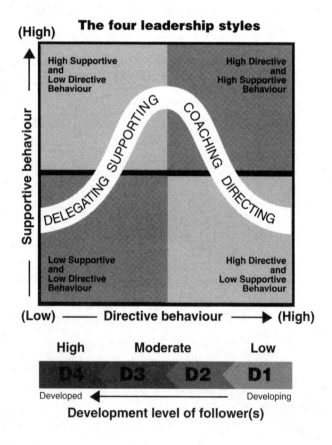

The four leadership styles

Development level of follower(s)

2. Which of the four styles do you think you practise the most (give examples where you can):

Directing:

- Giving instructions.
- Emphasising procedures and tasks.
- Acting firmly and quickly to correct errors.
- Closely supervising others.

Coaching:

- Working with others on joint problem-solving.
- Incorporating others' ideas into change.
- Ensuring everyone knows their responsibilities and expected standards.

Supporting:

- Helping others to feel important and involved.
- Giving help if asked, but not pushing.
- Encouraging others to work on problems.
- Getting others involved in determining roles and responsibilities.

Delegating:

- Intentionally not intervening.
- Letting others work out how to do things.
- Allowing a team to formulate its own plans.
- Giving broad direction and leaving them to get on with it.

3. Review whether your style is always appropriate

- Does it match the current development level of your reports?
- Do you vary it depending on the job in hand?
- Do you adapt it over time as individuals gain more experience and confidence?

- Do you move smoothly along the style curve or switch erratically from one extreme to the other?

4. How can you improve your situational leadership?

How it helps

To provide the most effective support and help to others, it is important to adapt your style to take account of their knowledge, experience and confidence. This tool uses a well-known model of leadership style to describe the four stages that can be used as individuals develop or situations change.

THERE IS NO 'RIGHT' STYLE TO USE –
THE KEY IS TO ADAPT TO INDIVIDUALS
AND SITUATIONS

Read Body Language

What it is

While words are important, nonverbal communication through the use of posture, movement and facial expression is very significant in really understanding how others feel. Albert Menabian found that the total impact of a message is 7% verbal (words only), 38% vocal (tone, inflection and other sounds) and 55% non verbal.

Nonverbal signals are often more genuine than words as they are harder to fake convincingly.

It may be that the skills of being perceptive, intuitive or able to relate well to others are based on the effective reading of body language.

This tool outlines a few aspects of body language as an instruction to the topic.

How to use it

1. Observe these positions and gestures.

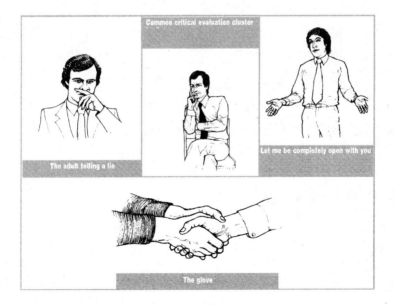

The adult telling a lie

Common critical evaluation cluster

Let me be completely open with you

The glove

These (and previous page) are some common things to look out for:

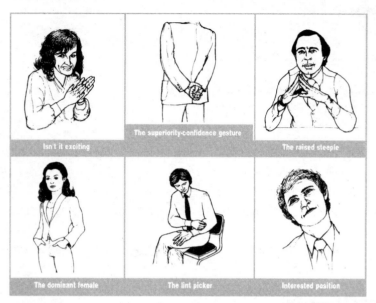

2. Do the gestures and postures you see, 'fit' with the words you hear?

3. What can you do to test your perception?

... 'you don't seem happy with my plan ...'

... 'this seems to be boring you ...'

... 'can you run through your proposal again ...'

... 'I'm not convinced you really agree with me ...'

4. If you still feel there is a lack of congruence between verbal and nonverbal; trust the body language, it's far harder to fake.

How it helps

Body language is a very significant communication medium. It is complex, however, and this tool can do no more than give a tiny taster of the subject.

For more detail refer to:
Body Language by Allan Pease ISBN 0-85969-782-7 Pbk

Be a Team Player

What it is

As John Donne said "No man is an island". However well you may perform as an individual there will be times when your success will be judged as a member of a team. This tool gives you ideas on how to be a successful team member.

How to use it

1. Think of a specific team to which you belong and answer the following questions – they will help you get to **GRIPS** with being a team member.

Goals

- Why does the team exist?
- What are the specific goals of the team?
- What are you expected to contribute?
- How will your success be measured?

Roles

- What role(s) do you play in the team? (technical expert/scribe/generating ideas/timekeeper etc)
- What do you need from the other members or the leader to fulfil your role?
- Do you share responsibility for the team's success?

Interactions

- Do you take part in team debates/meetings?
- Do you listen to others and ask questions?
- Do you build on others' ideas and contributions?
- Do you challenge others' views constructively?
- Do you contribute new ideas and information?
- Do you share your experiences?

Processes

- Are you clear how:

    - tasks are allocated?
    - decisions are made?
    - meetings are organised?
    - time is managed?
    - performance is reviewed and measured?
- Do you suggest how these processes can be improved?

Style

- Do you adapt your style to the team?

    - if you like to lead are you prepared to follow?
    - if you like structure and order can you cope with freeflowing creativity?
    - if you enjoy a fast pace, can you slow down to travel with others?
    - if you like facts can you work with feelings?

2. Go back to the questions you couldn't answer.

- Do you need to get some information?
- Do you need to seek feedback from other members?
- Do you need to think through why you're in the team?
- Do you need to plan how to improve your behaviour in the team?

3. What are you going to do to get to **GRIPS** with being a team member?

How it helps

This tool will help you to get briefed, prepared and organised to contribute successfully to a team even if it is not your natural environment.

REMEMBER – TEAMS CAN ACHIEVE FAR MORE THAN INDIVIDUALS IF EVERYONE PULLS IN THE SAME DIRECTION

Help others achieve

What it is

There will be times when your success will be judged not by what you do but by what you help others to achieve. This tool will help you to get to **GRIPS** with achieving results through other individuals.

How to use it

1. Think of a particular individual you are responsible for, and answer the following questions:

✔ Goals

- Does s/he have clear objectives to achieve?
- Have you agreed performance measures and targets?
- Is it clear how these 'fit' into the wider organisation?
- Have you been **SMART** (**S**pecific, **M**easurable, **A**chievable, **R**elevant and **T**imebound)?
- Do you regularly review progress, not just once a year at appraisal time?
- Do you tackle any gaps in performance promptly, looking for causes and solutions?

✔ Roles

- Does s/he feel clear about his/her role?
- Is your role clear?
- Have you swapped expectations?
- Does s/he understand how they fit into bigger processes?
- Are they appropriately empowered to make decisions?
- Is his/her job designed so they can control the resources for which they are responsible?

✔ <u>I</u>nteractions

- Do you give regular feedback on how they are doing?
- Do you seek regular feedback on how you are doing?
- Do you listen and act on their ideas and concerns?
- Do you involve him/her in discussions, decisions and new activities?

✔ **<u>P</u>ersonal development**

- Do you listen to his/her needs and wishes for development?
- Do you have an accurate picture of his/her knowledge, skills, experience and areas for improvement?
- Do you provide opportunities, both planned and spontaneous?
- Do you fund of-the-job training if needed?
- Do you encourage him/her to take responsibility for his/her own development?
- Do you spend time coaching him/her through new tasks and projects?
- Do you recognise his/her progress and success?
- Do you share your experiences?

✔ **<u>S</u>tyle**

- Do you manage everybody in the same way regardless of their experience or competence or do you adjust your style to fit their needs?
- Do you take account of the problem or issue to be tackled in choosing your style?
- Do you think through how much to involve others in the decisions to be made?

2. If you can answer yes to most of these questions you must already be an excellent coach, well done! You might like to test this however, by asking the individual concerned to give his/her view. If, however, you have spotted lots of gaps then decide which are the most significant and choose one or two to tackle initially.

3. Identify the steps you need to take to put them into practice.

How it helps

This tool will help you systematically plan and/or review your approach to helping others achieve by tackling the key areas of **GRIPS**.

HELPING OTHERS TO ACHIEVE ALSO INCREASES YOUR CHANCE OF SUCCESS

Recognise Success

What it is

The way in which people work is strongly influenced by the way leaders react. When working under pressure, it is easy to react only negatively when there are problems or poor results. However, if you want people to try new ways to experiment or take risks in order to improve performance, you must respond positively and constructively to their efforts as well as their results.

There are many ways in which recognition can be shown, both formal and informal.

This tool outlines a range of approaches to recognition for you to review and from which you can select.

How to use it

The following elements have all been incorporated successfully into formal recognition schemes by different companies.

- **Goals, measures, standards and targets**

  Unless performance is related back to the goals of the company/team/individual, there is no objective way of assessing whether recognition is appropriate.

  Crosfield (a UK chemical company) formally assess every OFI (Opportunity for Improvement) against the contribution to company goals and provide a range of responses.

- **Training and development**

  While basic training to do a job should be provided for everyone, attendance and achievement in training can be a useful form of recognition (certificates and presentations). Development through involvement in projects, visits, new tasks, deputising, etc is an ideal way of recognising earlier efforts.

  Everyone who goes on any training course at Milliken receives a certificate signed by Roger Milliken.

- **OFIs**

  Putting forward suggestions for improvement should always be recognised in some way. Many companies have formalised this by giving tokens, gifts or even financial reward in recognition of the number of OFIs contributed or benefits achieved.

  At Paul Revere Inc (US financial services) employees receive bronze, silver or gold badges for contributing 10, 25 or 50 improvement ideas.

- **Publicity**

  Perhaps the most common form of recognition is publicising achievements through notice-boards, storyboards, newsletters, presentations and word of mouth. The level of publicity can be linked to the size of achievement.

  The Japanese tend to be quite formal with their recognition relying mostly on the presidential review process to highlight teams with good stories. Through the year the process builds up through departments, then units, then locations reviewing short presentations. Finally, the best teams are invited to a conference attended by the president and top executives.

- **Tokens**

  Tokens can be provided to be given spontaneously for specific acts (not just by managers). Badges, key rings and mugs are common.

  At Clarke American, every employee has a recognition 'cheque book' and can complete a 'cheque' and give it to anyone in the company. Accumulated cheques can be exchanged for small gifts. This not only encourages recognition but develops contacts and relationships across the business.

- **Awards/events**

  Team/employee of the month/quarter/year are increasingly common. Clearly the criteria and method for assessment must be seen to be fair. Criteria can include customer employee feedback.

  Milliken take any opportunity to put the 'fans in the stands'. As well as awards such as 'quality project of the period' and 'associate of the month' they have sharing rallies at which improvement teams, OFI proposers and exceptional performers take a bow.

- **Sharing benefits**

  While recognition is not about financial reward, there are times when companies choose to share a proportion of any financial benefit achieved with those involved or donate it to charity. This can, however, be divisive and criteria must be very clearly defined.

- **Planned visits**

  Particularly where locations are split it is helpful for directors and managers to plan 'walking about'. Pre-briefing on OFIs, project teams, improvements achieved can make this a very powerful form of recognition. Do it often enough and it becomes the norm.

  Paul Revere has a PEET (Programme for Ensuring Everybody's Thanked) scheme which the Board uses to plan visits.

- **Everyday behaviour**

  Formal recognition will seem hollow and meaningless if not supported by day-to-day actions and behaviours. Informal, spontaneous recognition involves:

  - listening to ideas, suggestions, problems
  - encouraging and supporting involvement in improvement activities
  - being visible, accessible and approachable
  - having positive expectations about individual's

    ability and potential
  - understanding each individual's motivation needs and providing appropriate recognition for them
  - most of all giving praise and thanks for efforts, results and appropriate behaviour.

1. Review the various approaches to recognition. Which do you think would work for you?
2. Where will you start?
3. How will you go about it?
4. How will you ensure you are fair and consistent?

 RECOGNITION FEEDS FUTURE PERFORMANCE

How it helps

This tool identifies a range of approaches to recognition, both formal and informal and suggests ways in which you can help to make it happen.

Use Power and Influence

What it is

Your ability to have an impact on events will depend to a large extent on your ability to influence others to start or stop something or to do it differently. In turn, your ability to influence will be determined by the sources of power available to you.

This tool outlines the various types of power which can be used and helps you to diagnose your personal power net.

How to use it

In any relationship between two or more persons, each person will have different sources of 'power' over the others involved in the relationship.

Having an awareness of what 'power' you have in a particular relationship, at any particular moment in time can be very important. Similarly, having an awareness of what power the other person(s) has is equally important.

'Power' can be derived from a number of sources. Some examples of these sources are:

Expert   –   power derived from the person's expertise, technical skill or knowledge

Experiential   –   power derived from the person's previous experience

Status   –   they are the most senior person, and can 'order' you to do something

Charismatic   –   they have power derived from the strength of their personality

Referent   –   they obtain power by referring to someone else like an expert, their boss, or someone with a high status

Fear   –   they frighten people with physical aggression or personal threats.

1. What do you see as your sources of power?

2. Think of the most important people around you at work, What are their sources of power?

3. For each person you have described, how do you tend to influence each other?

4. Complete your power net diagram

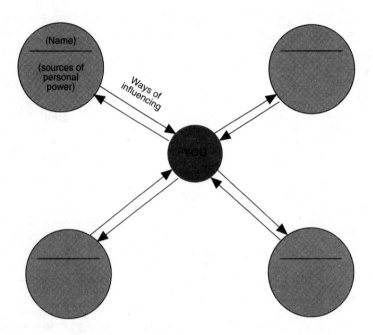

How it helps

This tool will help you to clarify the sources of power available to you and think how to use them to influence others around you.

6 Present yourself well

Look Good

What it is

Whether we like it or not, others judge us by how we look. Research shows that 90% of us make decisions about others in a few minutes. Over 50% of our personal impact is through our appearance, our body language and facial expressions. This tool gives you some practical tips on how to look good and create the right impression.

How to use it

1. Look at yourself in a full length mirror.

2. What do you see? Do a head to toe review:

   - Is your hair clean, styled and not obscuring your face?
   - Are your eyes clear and bright?
   - Are you smiling or scowling?
   - Are your clothes clean, neat and tidy or do you look as though you've slept in them?
   - Are your shoes clean and shining (however old)?
   - Are you standing tall or slouching?
   - Are you obviously overweight and unfit or do you look ready for action?
   - Are your eyes attracted to your face or to your clothes or jewellery?

3. So what do you feel you need to improve?

4. Use the following checklist to help you improve your dress and overall appearance:

Checklist on looking good (for business)

✔ Find a hairstyle that suits you and always keep your hair clean and well trimmed

✔ Find face creams or soaps that work for your skin – spots, dandruff or dry skin can be very off-putting

✔ Try to get enough sleep – nothing else works in the same way on your eyes and skin

✔ Use make-up to flatter and enhance not to mask or detract

WHEN YOU'RE JOINING A TEAM, IT HELPS TO WEAR THE SAME STRIP

✔ Wear appropriate business dress – if you're not sure what this is, ask or go and visit. For most companies it is still:

- fairly dark or neutral colours

- tailored jackets/suits

- black, grey or blue based rather than earthy colours

✔ Make the most of this 'uniform' by:

- choosing colours that suit you (are you winter, spring, summer or autumn? – get yourself 'colour-coordinated')

- wearing fabric types that suit you – natural fibres usually look better than synthetics

- being stylish but not too fashionable – classic clothes last longer and appeal to a wider audience

- not wearing heavy, dangling, garish jewellery – it attracts the eye away from your face

- even if your suit or jacket is cheap, wear a good quality shirt (and tie) or blouse – it's the most noticeable part of your outfit

- wear dark or neutral shoes – bright colours attract the eye away from your face

- use good quality accessories – briefcase, watch, diary, pen, etc – people usually notice

- consider wearing something memorable as your trade mark such as striking earrings or a pocket handkerchief – it will help others to remember you without being a misfit

- always ensure your shoes are clean and in good condition. Keep a spare pair in the car for driving to avoid the 'scuffed heel' look

- build a range of accessories – scarfs, bags, belts, jewellery, etc so you can change the appearance of a small number of outfits to match the occasion

✔ Be prepared to invest in your wardrobe – you might not like it but it pays dividends!

✔ Aim to dress 'a step up' from your peer group - you'll stand out and look successful

✔ If you are a hopeless case of bad taste, find a friend who can choose for you or talk to an 'image consultant'

✔ Look after your clothes, have them cleaned regularly, give them plenty of wardrobe space and mend any drooping hems, dangling buttons or tears

✔ If you don't need to wear business clothes, that's not an excuse to look a mess; choose appropriate casual outfits

✔ Don't expose too much skin – it detracts from your face and reduces credibility

✔ Buy the right size and fit. Nothing looks worse than bulging jackets or trousers at half mast

CHOOSE CLOTHES THAT FLATTER YOU BY THEIR COLOUR, TEXTURE AND FIT. LOOKING GOOD HELPS YOU TO FEEL GOOD

✔ Establish a self-maintenance routine – get your hair, teeth, nails and skin under control and looking good

✔ Do something about diet and exercise if posture and shape are your problem

✔ Don't wear strong perfume – tastes differ and the smell of roses to you may be lavatory cleaner to someone else

✔ Work on your body language:

- Don't sit all crossed and hunched – have a more open posture

- Don't fiddle with your hair/nails/clothes, etc. It suggests you're uncomfortable or nervous

- Practise a firm handshake, not a wet and weedy one

- Look people straight in the eye; smile but don't stare

- Don't touch people or stand too close – it invades their space and makes them uncomfortable

TRY WATCHING A VIDEO OF YOURSELF – YOU MIGHT GET A SURPRISE!

How it helps

Appearance counts. This tool will help you to look good at work, not in a fashion sense, but in a way that makes it more likely that others will listen to what you have to say.

 IF YOU LOOK GOOD, CHANCES ARE YOU'LL FEEL GOOD AND BE GOOD!

Sound Good

What it is

Sounding good is all about presenting yourself well in meetings and discussions. Research shows that our voice and how we speak accounts for nearly 40% of our personal impact. The content of what we say accounts for less than 10%. This tool outlines how to prepare and give a formal presentation as well as how to contribute to less formal discussions.

How to use it

1. If you have to give a presentation

- Decide aim, topic, title.
- Decide at what level to present – this depends upon
  - audience roles
  - audience knowledge.
- Collect relevant data:
  - search wide
  - read around the subject.
- Prepare broad framework of presentation:
  - introduction
  - content headings
  - conclusions
  - recommendations.
- Select and arrange appropriate data.
- Write presentation – some people write it all out in detail, others just use paragraph headings.
- Plan visual aid requirements – keep them simple:
  - overheads?
  - slides?
  - video?
  - handouts?

- Read through presentation to check logic.
- Check presentation room and facilities.
- Rehearse:
  - preferably with constructive companion
  - decide where and when to ask for questions
  - check timing.
- Deliver:
  - address all of the audience
  - be interesting.
- Confirm conclusions and actions.
- Review afterwards – how could it have been better?

2. If you have to attend a meeting

- Listen carefully to other views and ideas, don't spend all your time planning on what you want to say.
- Support and build on good ideas; don't put them down just because you're not sure how they would work.
- Don't talk over others; they won't be listening; say "can I just say something..." and wait for silence.
- Make sure you're sitting in the team, not out to one side so you can see and hear and be seen and heard.
- Input your views, experience, ideas as appropriate.
- Be clear, brief and to the point and then say "would you like more detail?/can I develop it further?"
- Question and constructively challenge others if they are unclear or appear illogical or irrelevant but don't be sarcastic – it's probably you who's confused!
- Get more actively involved by offering to scribe/keep notes/act as timekeeper. These jobs can increase your visibility and influence.
- Suggest tools that might help the team to be more effective and get everyone involved.

3. When using the telephone

- Stand up if you want to be more assertive.
- Smile if you want to sound warm and positive.
- Plan what you want to cover; jot down a list.
- Always say why you're calling.
- Use the other person's name.
- Take control of a call by giving it structure or bring it to a close – don't waste time or just chat.
- Take notes if you're being given information – you might think you'll remember but you probably won't. Read back anything where you might have misheard – such as phone numbers or addresses.
- Try to answer quickly – if you let it ring too long your caller is already unsettled.
- Don't be a silent listener – your voice is the only way the other person knows you're there.
- If the other person is upset or angry, just listen. Let them get it out of their system before you respond.

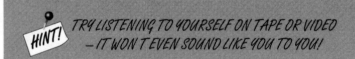

HINT! TRY LISTENING TO YOURSELF ON TAPE OR VIDEO – IT WON'T EVEN SOUND LIKE YOU TO YOU!

4. Finally, whatever the circumstances:

- avoid using too much jargon
- avoid using too many clichés
- speak clearly, don't mumble
- don't gabble
- temper your accent if it's very strong

- keep to the point
- sound (and be!) informed/experienced and confident
- don't hog the platform; give others a chance to speak too
- use gentle humour and anecdotes to make your point but avoid becoming a comic turn or causing offence.

How it helps

While appearance is important, words (and the visual aids you use to support them) are vital in communicating information and influencing others. This tool helps you to structure and present your views so you sound good and have substance.

Polish Your Curriculum Vitae

What it is

Your CV (Latin for 'course of life') is a summary of your qualifications, experience and skills. It is usually the key to getting a job interview (whether for an internal or external career move) and therefore must sell you well. This tool outlines the content of a good CV and how to put it together.

How to use it

1. Decide what information to include. The main headings are usually:

   ### Personal details

   • Name, address, contact number.

   ### Qualifications

   • School examination results (briefly).
   • Further education (subject(s), grades and location).
   • Vocational qualifications.

   ### Work experience

   • Dates, companies, brief job descriptions.
   • Responsibilities.
   • Achievements.
   • Skills acquired.

   ### Interests

   • Hobbies, sports, membership of organisations, charity or community work. Additional skills.

   ### Referees

   • Give two contact names.

2. Decide how to order the information

- **Chronological** – good for showing career progression, skill development. Start with most recent job.

- **Functional** – emphasises skills, abilities and achievements. More appropriate when looking to make a career change. Use headings such as Management, Project work; Marketing experience; Recruitment.

3. Decide on your presentation style

- Be eye-catching.

- Make it easy to skim-read.

- Use headings/boxes to break into sections.

- Keep it short and brief.

- Avoid too much jargon or too many management-speak terms (such as key or strategic).

4. Produce your CV to a high standard – good quality paper, a clear type face and no errors can really make a difference.

5. Ask someone else to review your CV for spelling, layout, clarity, etc and to pick up any obvious omissions or questions.

6. Review it yourself:

- Is it completely up to date?

- Is it honest and truthful?

- Are there things it would be better to omit?

- Would it help to expand slightly to give more detail?

- Does it emphasise achievements?

- Does it appeal to the particular reader?

7. Write an appropriate covering letter, highlighting why you are interested in or suitable for the particular role.

8. Amend your CV as necessary to ensure the best fit with a particular job by emphasising or expanding your most relevant experience.

9. Send it and wait for the invitation!

How it helps

In today's job market, a succinct, well-presented positive CV is vital to help you stand out from the crowd. Use this tool to help you get it right.

Interview Well

What it is

In these days of increasing job mobility it is likely that you will regularly have to sell yourself at interviews. This tool gives you tips on how to prepare and how to handle yourself at interviews.

How to use it

1. Before an interview

- Do your homework. Find out as much as you can about the company and the specific role. Most organisations will supply information on request but you can also use libraries, trade press, professional bodies, etc to do a search.

- Decide what you want to know about the organisation, job, package, etc. Write the questions down and take them with you – it's easy to forget in the heat of the moment.

- Make sure you are clear what is expected of you – ring up and ask if necessary. Often interviews are accompanied by tests and presentations.

- Take along relevant papers/samples/photos, etc which you can use to illustrate or explain your experience (but not too many, it's easy to overwhelm an interviewer).

- Make sure you know who is going to interview you in terms of their role(s) and relationship to the position you want.

HINT!

PRACTISE TALKING THROUGH YOUR CAREER HISTORY – IF YOU ARE ASKED TO EXPAND ON WHAT YOU'VE DONE OR ACHIEVED IN PARTICULAR ROLES, DON'T WAIT UNTIL THE INTERVIEW TO REMEMBER EVENTS OF YEARS AGO

- Think about the questions you might be asked – particularly if you are aware of gaps between your CV and the job requirements. How will you answer them?

- Decide what to wear – make sure it's clean! Interviewers normally expect formal, business dress.

- Check how to get to the interview and make sure you know how much time to allow.

- Make the necessary arrangements to be absent from your current role.

2. During an interview

- Turn up a few minutes early.

- Take off your coat (not suit jacket) and arrange your bags, etc so you can easily shake hands with the interviewer.

- Make sure you note who is who if there is more than one interviewer and try and remember names.

- Try and look reasonably relaxed. Don't screw yourself into a ball; have an open posture.

HINT!

MAKE PLENTY OF EYE CONTACT BUT DON'T STARE. SMILE!

- Answer the questions asked, expand but don't pontificate. You can always ask "would you like to know more ...?".

- Be prepared to offer extra information if you feel it helps or if the interviewer seems dissatisfied. You can always say "does that answer your question?" or "you don't seem happywith that".

- Be ready to ask the questions you prepared and any others that have occurred to you. Don't expect nitty-gritty answers on points of detail if this is a preliminary interview.

- At the end ask, "have you found out everything you wanted?" or if you're really bold "how do you feel the interview has gone" or "do you have any doubts about whether I could do the job?".

3. After an interview

- If you get the job, well done, celebrate!

- If you didn't, why not ring and ask for some feedback to help you next time?

- Sometimes it's appropriate to write a short note of thanks if the interviewer was particularly helpful.

How it helps

Interviews are the doorway to new opportunities and challenges. This tool will help you pass through as painlessly as possible.

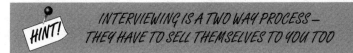

HINT!

INTERVIEWING IS A TWO WAY PROCESS — THEY HAVE TO SELL THEMSELVES TO YOU TOO

Radiate Energy

What it is

Energy is contagious. The more energy you have, the more you will demonstrate this to others; the better you feel about what you do, the more others will sense this and choose to align with you. This tool outlines the behaviours that demonstrate energy and helps you to identify how to increase and radiate your energy.

How to use it

1. Energy is demonstrated and radiated in the following ways:

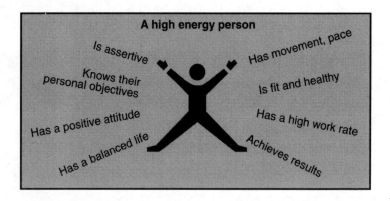

A high energy person

Is assertive

Knows their personal objectives

Has a positive attitude

Has a balanced life

Has movement, pace

Is fit and healthy

Has a high work rate

Achieves results

- Use the following questions to assess your energy level:

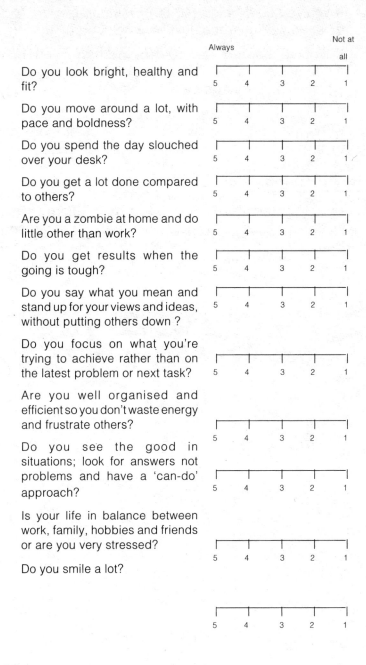

	Always				Not at all
Do you look bright, healthy and fit?	5	4	3	2	1
Do you move around a lot, with pace and boldness?	5	4	3	2	1
Do you spend the day slouched over your desk?	5	4	3	2	1
Do you get a lot done compared to others?	5	4	3	2	1
Are you a zombie at home and do little other than work?	5	4	3	2	1
Do you get results when the going is tough?	5	4	3	2	1
Do you say what you mean and stand up for your views and ideas, without putting others down ?	5	4	3	2	1
Do you focus on what you're trying to achieve rather than on the latest problem or next task?	5	4	3	2	1
Are you well organised and efficient so you don't waste energy and frustrate others?	5	4	3	2	1
Do you see the good in situations; look for answers not problems and have a 'can-do' approach?	5	4	3	2	1
Is your life in balance between work, family, hobbies and friends or are you very stressed?	5	4	3	2	1
Do you smile a lot?	5	4	3	2	1

2. Work out your total score:

If you've scored high (40-60), well done, your batteries must be well charged; just beware of burn out!

If you've scored low (0-19), perhaps you need to fundamentally to review what you're doing; you may well be stressed and unhappy.

If you're in the middle (20-39), then pick out the areas where your score is low and use the other more specific tools in this Toolbox to identify improvements.

How it helps

You will only radiate energy if you have energy. This tool identifies a range of behaviours which are both symptoms and sources of energy and helps you to assess how well you demonstrate them. Other tools can then be used to tackle weak areas.

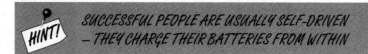

HINT!

SUCCESSFUL PEOPLE ARE USUALLY SELF-DRIVEN — THEY CHARGE THEIR BATTERIES FROM WITHIN

Focus Energy

What it is

The TUFF task checklist, based on

Think – **U**nderstand – **F**ocus – **F**inish,

is designed to help you to focus your energy when faced with a problem to solve or a situation to improve.

How to use it

1. Review the TUFF task checklist (next page).

2. Apply each step to the particular problem or situation you're working on.

3. Review your success and identify how you could do even better.

4. Put your idea into practice on your next TUFF task.

How it helps

The TUFF task checklist will help you tackle problems and make changes in a systematic and managed way by ensuring you **T**hink – **U**nderstand – **F**ocus – **F**inish

THINK

Think big...
dream freely...
find the best idea

- what can we do to make a big difference?
- is this a breakthrough?
- are there other alternatives... other solutions?
- what will it take to make it happen?
- imagine the end result... visualise the impact

'If you can dream it, you can make it so.'

UNDERSTAND

Challenge your idea...
use your judgement...

- test your new concept... research, get data, analyse
- set an objective and break it down into achievable chunks
- plan the action through to completion, with milestones
- estimate and quantify the changes, the resources, the costs
- communicate the concept and the plan to all affected

'Failing to plan is planning to fail'

FOCUS

Drive it hard...
make progress quickly ...
don't let inertia sap your energy

- be clear about your priorities... you can only handle three or four TUFFTASKS at a time
- keep it simple and uncluttered... don't over-engineer
- what can you stop doing to make space for this?
- build a small team and lead it actively
- delegate sub-tasks but stay close... inspire people to deliver

'Obstacles are the things you see when you take your eye off the goal'

FINISH!!!

Don't stop until it's done...
be immune to distraction and routine...
keep the inspiration up... this is exciting!!!

- test it... are you getting there?
- work on the details yourself... success is often in the details
- be determined... creativity needs your energy to make it happen
- communicate again... let people know all about it
- make sure it's used... don't let go until it is fully working
- celebrate, be proud... then move on, there's more still to achieve

'Nothing has value until it is finished'

Ride the Roller Coaster

What it is

In planning and implementing change, it is important to be aware and take account not only of the hard facts, figures, resources, etc but also to consider the emotional response of those involved.

The Change Curve illustrates the typical sequence of emotions that we experience when faced with change.

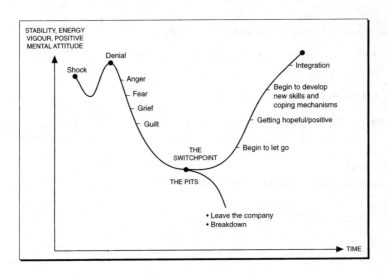

How to use it

The emotional roller-coaster of change will happen whether we like it or not. You can help others (and yourself) to move through it relatively quickly and painlessly by:

1. Communicating

- Communicate plans and goals as soon as possible, always explaining why they are necessary.

- Keep everyone up-to-date as things progress – if you don't, the grapevine will.

- Ensure communication is two–way. LISTEN to concerns and views. Pass on feedback and questions as appropriate. Answer as many questions as you can and always be honest.

2. Listening and counselling

- Give individuals the opportunity to talk to you privately about how they will be affected.

- Give time and space for individuals to reflect, absorb and come to terms with change as it affects them.

- Make it clear it's OK to voice concerns and fears.

3. Coaching and developing

- Work with individuals to help them to develop the knowledge and skills needed in the new environment.

4. Involving

- Get individuals involved in planning and implementing change so they feel a sense of ownership over what's happening.

5. Energising and enthusing

- By your own approach, style and energy encourage others to be positive and enthusiastic.

- Show confidence and be confident by satisfying yourself of the whats, whys and hows.

- Look for answers, not problems. Tackle blockages constructively.

How it helps

Helping individuals through their emotional reactions to change, accelerates the pace at which it can be introduced and increases the likelihood of success.

Be Creative

What it is

Creativity is the process of generating new ideas. While we may not all see ourselves as budding inventors or innovative thinkers there are some very practical things we can do to help ourselves and others to increase our creativity.

This tool outlines a range of actions which together will help to open up your mind.

How to use it

1. Review the ideas on how to encourage creativity below.

2. Identify the things you feel you already do. Be specific. Give examples.

3. Identify the areas you've never thought of tackling. Which ones appeal to you most?

4. How could you put them into practice in your work or your area?

5. Be creative in how you go about it!

 REMEMBER: IF YOU ALWAYS DO WHAT YOU'VE ALWAYS DONE, YOU'LL ALWAYS GET WHAT YOU'VE ALWAYS GOT

How to encourage creativity

✔ **Clarify objectives**

- Lift your eyes to your ultimate goal; focus on the benefits; imagine what it will be like

- Be honest and realistic about measures, constraints and resources, but see these as opportunities to do things differently

- Be demanding – it can force a new approach to working smarter not harder

✔ **Set groundrules**

- Agree when it's OK to take risks; make changes
- Clarify if and when you expect new ideas
- Remove existing norms if appropriate (eg a proposal must always be cost justified before being presented)
- Take calculated risks to give freedom for innovation

✔ **Manage the environment**

- Move away from the 'normal' work environment
- Use colours, music, smells to generate ideas
- Create quiet 'thinking' places
- Make work fun and enjoyable (as well as demanding); too much stress and tension reduce creativity
- Encourage breaks – fresh air, movement, exercise and healthy food can stimulate thinking

✔ **Use mixed media**

- People respond differently to different methods, so use a mixture
- Don't always rely on words to stimulate others
- Use pictures, sounds, touch to get across messages or to receive ideas
- Work with emotions as well as logical thoughts

✔ **Suspend your judgement**

- Be open-minded to new ideas
- Listen
- Develop other ideas before assessing them
- Look for positives, not just problems ('yes but..')
- Don't expect others to think or to express themselves as you do

✔ Use problem solving tools

- Use brainstorming and mindmapping to open up possibilities

- Use the other tools in the *Solve that problem!* Toolbox to analyse options and plan actions

✔ Use teams

- Create a supportive yet demanding culture to encourage free expression and exploration

- Ensure members challenge the assumptions and perceptions of others

- Share experiences to broaden horizons

- Combine knowledge and skills to open up new ways

- Hold 'what if' meetings to 'imagine' an alternative future:

    - identify options, implications and impact

    - clarify what resources would be needed

    - assess the benefits

    - test ideas (where, how, what, etc)

    - only reject ideas at the point you're sure they won't work

✔ Challenge paradigms

- Use benchmarking to challenge assumptions about what can be done

- Visit other sites/departments/industries, etc to see different approaches

- Move people around to encourage a 'fresh pair of eyes'

- Stop and analyse the values, prejudices and assumptions that you (and others) have which colour your judgement... test whether they are appropriate

✔ Think 'actively'

- Don't just accept 'facts' passively (like watching the TV)

- Push yourself to think of alternatives; see things from the opposite point of view: do things a different way

- Make comparisons to highlight patterns, similarities or differences

- Learn to learn – set yourself development goals; take on new challenges; review yourself; seek feedback

✔ Think positively

- Have confidence in your ability to innovate

- Use your power to the full

- Believe in your own abilities and strengths – identify what they are and how you can build on them

- Have a 'can do' approach to problems; 'if you think you can, you will'

- Be 'out there' – getting out and about and just making yourself available for people to raise questions/issues – **THEN** picking them up and getting them answered/dealt with – proactive facilitation if you like!

- Pick up on 'wild/off-the-wall ideas' – get in touch with the 'irrational'. Encourage people to bring these ideas to you, develop them with them, create something do-ablefrom them

- Don't ask why; ask why not!. Dream it, do it, involve people

✔ Learn from mistakes

- What happened?
- Why?
- What were/are the implications?
- What could be different next time?

How it helps

You can't have a new brain (yet!), but you can develop the one you've got to be more creative. This tool gives a range of practical actions you can take to increase your own and others' creativity.

Manage Stress

What it is

Stress is the body's automatic response to challenge and change. Up to a point, it is very positive and improves performance; once past this point, however, it will reduce performance and ultimately lead to anxiety and depression if not tackled.

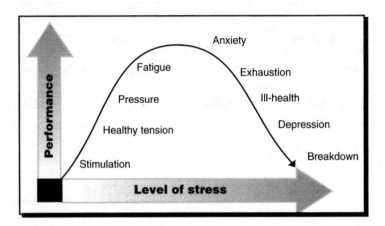

Stress can be caused by:

- our environment, eg noise, heat

- work, eg overload, lack of objectives, ambiguity, continual change

- other people, eg aggression, discrimination, family, lack of contact

- ourselves, eg lack of exercise, poor diet, health, money, ambitions, self-image.

This tool will help you to assess your current stress level and identify any typical symptoms you may have. It then goes on to give some tips on how to manage your stress.

How to use it

Researchers, Holmes and Rahe devised a 'Social Readjustment Scale' which listed events in our lives which are rated according to the amount of adjustment required. They found that 80% of people who ran up over 300 points in one year were at risk of illness in the near future. Of those people who scored 155-299 points, 50% soon became ill, and of those with less than 150 stress points, 3% became ill shortly after the life events.

1. Use the Holmes and Rahe ratings scale to assess your current stress level.

2. Add up your own score, based on events in your life during the past year. But if your score is high, don't panic. Not everyone will become ill after a considerable amount of change – personality and previous experience of coping will enable some people to ride over it all without serious problems. But it is as well to be aware of the possible effects of changes in your life, and to look out for signs of stress.

Social readjustment rating scale

Event	Life crises – unit score
Death of wife or husband	100
Divorce	73
Marital separation	65
Prison sentence	63
Death of close family member	63
Personal injury or illness	53
Marriage	50
Getting the sack from work	47
Marital reconciliation	45
Retirement	45
Change in health of family member	44
Pregnancy	40
Addition of new family member	39
Major business problems	39
Change in financial state	38
Death of close friend	37
Change to different kind of work	36
Taking on a large mortgage	31
Foreclosure of mortgage or loan	30
Change in responsibilities at work	29
Son or daughter leaving home	29
Outstanding personal achievement	28
Spouse starts/stops work	26
Change in living conditions	25
Revision of personal habits	24
Trouble with the boss	23
Change in working hours or conditions	20
Change in residence	20
Change in recreation	19
Change in church activities	19
Change in social activity	18
Taking on a bank loan or HP debt	17
Change in sleeping habits	16
Change in eating habits	15
Holiday	13
Minor violations of the law	11

3. Review the symptoms of anxiety and depression and highlight any you are experiencing:

Anxiety

Private signs

inability to concentrate
increase in alcohol consumed
increase in smoking
increase in eating
inability to unwind
tenseness
confusion
loss of sleep – inability to get to sleep
agitation, restlessness
hyperactiveness
panic

Public signs

distractibility
exaggeration of trivia
irritability
indecisiveness
'tunnel vision'
indiscriminate blaming
always taking work home
bad driving
garrulousness (wordy)
capriciousness (whimsical)
exaggerated sense of own indispensability

Depression

Private signs

decline in sexual interest
increase in alcohol consumed
weariness
poor memory
'weary dissatisfaction'
lack of confidence
feelings of abandonment
loss of sleep – inability to get to sleep
feelings of rejection
despondency, pessimism
resentment

Public signs

inertia
uncontrollable mood swings
social withdrawal
apathy
indecisiveness
suspiciousness
lying
absenteeism
slow response
disinterest
resentment
low productivity

Psychosomatic signs

Skin irritations, vague aches and pains, recurrence of previous illnesses, generally feeling 'one degree under', headaches, breathing difficulty, excessive sweating.

Please note: such lists are useful only for **describing** something that is happening. The crucial test is **change** in the individual concerned relative to his/her "normal self".

4. Use the following checklist on Managing Stress to identify actions you can take:

✔ Take up some form of exercise

✔ Learn a relaxation technique

✔ Ensure your diet is balanced and healthy

✔ Get some fresh air

✔ Build short breaks into your day

✔ Clarify your goals and priorities, at home as well as work

✔ Get organised

✔ Know your own strengths and limitations and accept yourself as you are

✔ Get problems out in the open and search for solutions. Don't bottle it all up behind a brave face

✔ Aim for variety in your life and work

✔ 'Do it now!'; taking action or making decisions will at least partly remove tension

✔ Address problems in relationships; use third parties to help if necessary

✔ Cut down on alcohol and tobacco

✔ Laugh at yourself (it's better than crying!)

✔ Make the most of your holidays – have a real break; do something different

✔ Recognise your symptoms and sources of stress and accept you need to do something about it

---

How it helps

Stress can get in the way and waste energy that you could use far better for other things. Use this tool to highlight your current stress level and identify practical steps you can take to reduce it.

 REMEMBER: EVERYONE IS DIFFERENT. THE SAME SITUATION CAN CAUSE ONE PERSON TO THRIVE AND ANOTHER TO WILT. KNOW WHAT'S RIGHT FOR YOU!